Networking Without the BS

Richard Lowe

The Writing King

Networking Without the BS

Copyright © 2026 by Richard G Lowe

Although every precaution has been taken to verify the accuracy of the information contained herein, the author and publisher assume no responsibility for any errors or omissions. No liability is assumed for damages that may result from the use of information contained within.

Trademarked names appear throughout this book. Rather than use a trademark symbol with every occurrence of a trademarked name, names are used in an editorial fashion, with no intention of infringement of the respective owner's trademark.

Table of Contents

See books by Richard Lowe at

https://masterofworlds.com

Get free publishing insights and industry updates at

https://thewritingking.substack.com

For ghostwriting and book coaching services see

https://thewritingking.com

Preface

I was terrible at networking. For most of my career, I kept my head down, did my work, and avoided the social aspects of business. I thought networking was for slick salespeople and smooth talkers, not introverted computer guys like me.

I got by with this method until circumstances changed.

During my time as the Computer Operations Director at Trader Joe's, I managed the computer systems for a multi-billion-dollar company with a skeleton crew. Corporate policy strictly limited our headcount, so when major problems hit, we were on our own.

One Friday night, our primary system crashed. Not a minor glitch, but a complete failure that could cost the company millions if it wasn't fixed by Monday morning. I spent hours trying everything I knew, then calling every vendor number I could find. Most didn't answer after business hours. Those who did treated me just like another customer who could wait until Monday.

I sat in that empty office, surrounded by broken computers, realizing I had no one to call for help. Twenty years in the industry, and I had built exactly zero meaningful professional relationships. I was completely alone when I needed help most.

The crash eventually got fixed through sheer determination and sleepless nights, but it taught me a harsh lesson. Technical skills weren't enough. I needed people who knew me, trusted me, and would go out of their way to help when everything went wrong.

So I started building relationships. Awkwardly at first. I went to conferences and forced myself to talk to strangers. I joined professional groups and took part instead of just attending. I followed up with people even when I didn't need anything from them.

Slowly, my network grew. A few years later, when another major crisis hit, I made a handful of calls and had a team of experts working on the problem within hours. Not because I paid them, but because we had genuine relationships built over time.

When I left Trader Joe's to become a writer, I faced the same problem all over again. I couldn't network my way out of a paper bag in the writing and publishing worlds. I knew nothing about book marketing, publishing, or building an author platform. Once again, I had to learn from scratch.

This time, I applied the networking lessons I was learning. I joined writing groups, connected with other authors, and slowly built a network that supported my new career. The principles were the same, but the application was completely different.

That's why I wrote this book. Not because I'm a networking guru who was born knowing how to work a room, but because I learned these skills the hard way through trial and error, embarrassing mistakes, and hard-won experience.

If an introverted computer geek can learn to build meaningful professional relationships, anyone can. The key is understanding that networking doesn't mean being smooth or manipulative. It's about genuinely helping other people and building authentic relationships for the long term.

Most business owners either avoid networking entirely or do it completely wrong. Both approaches limit growth and opportunity. This book shows you what works, based on real experience rather than theory.

Introduction

I stumbled into my first networking success completely by accident, which probably explains why it took me decades to understand what had happened.

During college, I was the classic introvert. I kept my head down, did my work, and avoided asking for help unless I was desperate. When I needed something from teachers or administrators, they barely knew who I was. Why would they go out of their way for some random student they'd never bothered to know?

Despite keeping to myself, I landed my first job straight out of college at a small startup company as its first employee. Looking back, I realize this happened because of networking, but at the time I had no clue.

My best friend Don and I spent most of our time in the computer lab working on assignments. Unknown to us, Mr. James, the department head, was watching us work.

Mr. James had been working with one of our teachers, Fred, a seven-foot-tall giant who had started a company helping businesses install computer systems. In those days, computers filled entire rooms and disk drives were the size of washing machines.

When Fred offered to sponsor a student to attend the biggest computer convention of the year, Mr. James jumped at the opportunity and recommended Don for the small travel stipend. Don didn't want to go alone, so he invited me along. I didn't know what I was getting into, but since Don was covering all the expenses with his stipend money, I agreed.

At the convention, Fred invited us to dinner with his business partners and four of the most influential people in the computer industry. These were the guys who had designed the first programming languages for Digital Equipment Corporation. They were legends.

I sat at that dinner table like a fish out of water stranded on a high mountain in the desert. How could I even talk to these people? I didn't know what to say, so I mostly listened and tried not to embarrass myself.

A month later, Fred called and offered me a job as his first employee. I found out later that Mr. James had recommended me over every other student in the department. Fred had been watching my work based on that recommendation, and the dinner conversation had convinced him to take a chance on me.

That three-hour dinner changed everything. Within days, I dropped out of college, moved 100 miles, and started my career in the computer industry. I went from student to vice president of consulting within a year, later moved to Beck Computer Systems in the same role, and eventually became Computer Operations Director at Trader Joe's for 20 years.

All because of one dinner where I barely said anything.

The problem was I learned nothing from this experience. I didn't follow up with any of those industry heavyweights. I didn't realize that relationships had opened that door for me. I just assumed I had gotten lucky or that my technical skills had impressed someone. But I did collect dozens and dozens of business cards!

When I started my computer career, I didn't even try to build professional relationships. My shyness and complete lack of social skills kept me isolated. I focused entirely on the technical work and ignored the human side of business.

My boss had tried to show me the value of networking through his own example, but I was too stubborn and arrogant to pay attention. The job eventually forced me out of my shell because the responsibilities were too big for one person to handle alone. I had to learn to delegate, manage, and eventually reach out to others for help and advice.

Slowly, I began building relationships with other professionals. As my network grew, everything became easier. Instead of struggling alone, I could connect with talented people who knew, liked, and trusted me. They were eager to help because we had genuine relationships, not just business card exchanges.

When I left Trader Joe's to become a writer, I faced the same networking challenge all over again. This time, I applied what I had learned about relationship building, even though I was still awkward at it.

This book shares the lessons I learned the hard way. I'm not a natural networker who was born knowing how to work a room. I'm an introvert who had to figure out these skills through trial and error, embarrassing mistakes, and painful experiences.

If someone as socially clueless as I was can learn to build meaningful professional relationships, anyone can. The key is understanding that networking doesn't involve being smooth or manipulative. It's about genuinely helping other people and building authentic relationships.

Chapter 1: What is Networking?

Many professionals mistakenly believe networking is schmoozing at cocktail parties or glad-handing at Chamber of Commerce mixers. They imagine smooth talkers at events, gathering contacts and using quick speeches to impress people they don't know.

That's garbage. That's performance art, not networking.

Effective networking comes down to developing authentic professional partnerships. That's it. People helping people they know, like, and trust.

"People network because they want to meet people, and build a relationship, and collaborate, and do business with..." -
Haleh Houshim

Here's a simple example. Your house needs painting, but you've heard horror stories about contractors who disappear with deposits, do shoddy work, or leave projects half-finished. You don't want to pick someone randomly from Google, so you ask your friend Bill if he knows any talented painters.

Bill doesn't personally know any painters, but he reaches out to his network. He calls his neighbor who recently had work done, checks with his brother-in-law who works in construction, and asks a couple of colleagues if they have recommendations. Within a day, Bill gets back to you with a painter that three different people vouched for.

When you call that painter, you don't start as a stranger begging to get squeezed into his schedule. You start with "Bill referred me to you." Immediately, you're not just another cold call. You're connected to people the painter knows and trusts.

If the painter does good work, everyone wins. You get a quality paint job, Bill feels good about helping a friend, and the painter gets a satisfied customer who might refer others. If something goes wrong, there's accountability because the painter's reputation with multiple people is at stake.

That's networking in action. No business cards were exchanged. No elevator pitches delivered. No one worked the room. Just people helping people through relationships built over time.

The power multiplies because each person in your network has their own network. When I need help with something outside my expertise, I can tap into not just the dozen people I know well, but potentially hundreds of people they know.

During my years at Trader Joe's, I maintained relationships with dozens of people in the computer industry. I didn't hire most of them or buy from their companies, but I stayed in touch regularly. When I faced a problem I couldn't solve alone, I could reach out to this network and usually find someone who either had the answer or knew someone who did.

A few years later, we had another major system failure. This time, I made a few phone calls to people I'd built relationships with over the years. Within hours, I had experts working on the problem because we had genuine professional relationships.

This is completely different from transactional relationships where you only contact people when you need something. In real networking, you invest time in relationships long before you need help. You stay in touch, offer help when they need it, and build trust.

"Networking in business is the process of creating and maintaining mutually beneficial relationships with other business people." – Mark O'Donnell

---

Here's where most people screw this up. They think networking is about what they can get from other people. Wrong. It's about what you can give. When you consistently help others solve problems, make connections, and achieve their goals, they naturally want to help you in return. Not because they owe you, but because humans are wired to reciprocate kindness.

Many business owners approach networking backward. They show up at events hunting for customers, partners, or opportunities without first building relationships. They focus on what they need instead of what they can offer. This feels pushy and rarely produces lasting results.

Effective networking requires a longer view. You meet people, learn about their challenges and goals, and look for ways to help them succeed. You stay in touch regularly, not just when you need something. You build genuine professional friendships based on mutual respect.

This doesn't mean networking is slow. Sometimes you can help someone immediately, and they remember when an opportunity comes up that's perfect for you. But the strongest networks are built through consistent effort over months, years, and even decades, not through one-time interactions at networking events.

The other crucial element is authenticity. People can sense when you're genuinely interested in helping them versus when you're trying to manipulate them for your own benefit. Authentic networking feels natural and builds lasting relationships. Manipulative networking feels forced and creates surface-level connections that disappear when you need them most.

Modern networking happens both online and offline. You might meet someone at a conference, connect with them on LinkedIn, and stay in touch through occasional messages. Or you might build relationships entirely through online communities and video calls. The medium doesn't matter. The authenticity of the connection does.

Focus on creating genuine value for others, and opportunities naturally emerge. People think of you when they hear about jobs, partnerships, speaking opportunities, or other possibilities that match your interests and skills.

This shift in mindset changes everything. Instead of dreading networking events as sales competitions, you can approach them as opportunities to meet interesting people and learn about their work. Instead of collecting business cards to add to your database, you can focus on making meaningful connections with a few people who share your interests or face similar challenges.

The businesses that grow fastest and weather storms best are usually run by people who understand this principle. They invest time in building relationships throughout their industry, not just with customers but with peers, suppliers, advisors, and even competitors. When they need help, resources, or opportunities, they have a network of people who are genuinely interested in their success.

This is the true power of networking. It's not about socializing with people or having the best pitch. It's about building authentic relationships that create value for everyone involved. When you master this approach, business becomes easier, more enjoyable, and far more successful than you thought possible.

Recap

Networking is building genuine relationships with other professionals who can help you solve problems and find opportunities. It works through people helping people they know, like, and trust. The foundation is giving help and value to others before you need anything in return. Effective networking focuses on authenticity and long-term relationship building instead of short-term transactions. Both online and offline networking follow the same basic principles of creating genuine value for others.

Exercise

Think about a recent problem you solved or opportunity you discovered. Trace back how you found the solution or learned about the opportunity. Did it come through a personal connection, a referral, or someone you knew? Most business success comes through relationships instead of cold outreach or advertising. Recognizing this pattern in your own experience will help you understand why networking is essential for business growth.

Chapter 2: It's About Relationships

I learned about the power of relationships by watching my boss Steve operate. While I was buried in technical manuals and computer code, Steve was having lunch meetings with people who seemed to have nothing to do with our business.

At first, I thought he was wasting time. These weren't vendor meetings or client presentations. They were casual conversations over coffee with people from other companies, other industries, other states. Steve would spend two hours talking about sports, family, business trends, and whatever else came up. I couldn't see the point.

I was wrong. Steve wasn't wasting time. He was investing in relationships.

This became clear during one of our worst technical crises. We had a client whose system had crashed in a way none of us had ever seen. Our entire team was stumped. We'd tried everything we knew, called every vendor in our contact database, and brought in outside consultants. Nothing worked.

The client was furious. They were losing money every hour the system stayed down, and we were running out of ideas. I was panicking about losing the account.

Steve made one phone call. He reached out to someone he'd had lunch with six months earlier, a guy who worked for a completely different company in another state. That person didn't have the answer, but he knew someone who did. Within four hours, we had a specialist on site who solved the problem in thirty minutes.

The specialist didn't charge us emergency rates. He didn't even send us a bill. He fixed our problem because Steve had asked for help, and people who know Steve want to help him. All he asked was for us to remember him for future business and to cover his expenses.

That's when I began to understand what networking means. It's not about collecting business cards or attending mixers. It's about building relationships with people who will help you when everything falls apart.

Steve had invested time in getting to know that guy over lunch. They'd talked about their businesses, their challenges, their goals. Steve had offered to help if the guy ever needed anything, and he'd followed up periodically to stay in touch. When Steve needed help, that relationship paid off in ways no amount of money could have bought.

The key word here is relationship. Not contact. Not connection. Relationship.

A contact is someone whose business card you collected. A connection is someone you met at an event or added on LinkedIn. A relationship is someone who knows you, likes you, and trusts you enough to go out of their way to help when you're in trouble, and you would gladly do the same for them.

Most people confuse networking with collecting contacts. They go to events, tap their phones together to gather names and phone numbers, add people to their database, and think they're building a network. Wrong. They're building a list of strangers who might remember meeting them once.

Real networking is about building relationships that create mutual value. It's about getting to know people as human beings, not just as potential customers or vendors. It's about offering help without keeping score or expecting immediate returns.

This takes time. You can't build relationships in a quick conversation. You build them through regular contact, genuine interest in the other person's success, and consistent follow-through. Building a network isn't speed dating. It takes time and effort.

After watching Steve in action, I started approaching networking differently. Instead of focusing on what I could get from people, I focused on what I could give. Instead of trying to impress people with my technical knowledge, I tried to understand their challenges and see how I might help.

I started having lunch meetings with people in my industry. Not to sell them anything or ask for anything, but to get to know them and their businesses. I learned about their problems, their goals, their successes and failures. I offered advice when I could, made introductions when appropriate, and stayed in touch regularly.

Slowly, my network grew. Not my contact list, but my actual network of people who knew me and trusted me. When I needed help with a technical problem, I had people to call. When I heard about opportunities that might benefit someone in my network, I passed them along.

I wasn't doing this enough, but I was making the right moves. Even the little I was doing transformed my career. Instead of struggling alone with every challenge, I had access to hundreds of years of combined experience from people who were genuinely interested in helping me succeed.

The relationships I built during those startup years stayed with me throughout my career. When I moved to Beck Computer Systems, some of those same people helped me transition. When I joined Trader Joe's, my network provided resources and advice that made me more effective.

Years later, when I changed careers, I faced the same challenge in a completely different industry. I slowly began applying the same relationship-building principles.

I joined writing groups and participated instead of just attending. I connected with other authors and offered to help promote their work. I built relationships with editors, book cover designers, and marketing professionals. I shared what I learned about self-publishing and asked for advice about areas where I was struggling.

The writing community welcomed me because I approached it with the right attitude. I wasn't trying to use people to advance my career. I was trying to build genuine relationships with people who shared similar interests and challenges.

This is the fundamental difference between networking that works and networking that doesn't. When you focus on building relationships, opportunities naturally emerge. People think of you when they hear about jobs, partnerships, or other possibilities that might interest you.

When you focus on extracting value from people, they sense your agenda and keep their distance. They might be polite, but they won't go out of their way to help you. They certainly won't refer their friends to you.

The businesses that grow fastest and survive longest are built on relationships, not transactions. The professionals who advance furthest in their careers are usually those who invest time in building genuine connections with others in their field.

You shouldn't be calculating about relationships or keep a mental scorecard of who owes whom. That defeats the purpose. Authentic relationships are built on genuine care for other people's success.

You help people because you want to help them, not because you expect something in return. You stay in touch because you're interested in their lives and businesses, not because you're hunting for opportunities. You offer value because it feels good to contribute to other people's success.

When you approach networking with this mindset, everything changes. People can sense your authenticity, and they respond to it. They want to help you because they know you would help them. They refer opportunities to you because they trust your character and competence.

This is why relationship-based networking is so much more powerful than transactional networking. It's built on trust, mutual respect, and genuine human connection. It creates lasting value for everyone involved, and it gets stronger over time.

The time and effort you invest in building relationships always pays dividends, though not always in ways you expect. The person you help today might refer a major client to you next year. The advice you give to someone in your network might come back to you transformed into an opportunity you never could have imagined.

This is the real secret of successful networking. It's not about socializing or adding contacts to your address book. It's about building authentic relationships with people who can help you achieve your goals while you help them achieve theirs.

Recap

Networking is about building genuine relationships, not collecting contacts or connections. Authentic relationships require time, effort, and genuine interest in other people's success. Focus on what you can give instead of what you can get. Invest time in getting to know people as human beings, not just as potential business opportunities. Relationships built on trust and mutual respect create lasting value and get stronger over time.

Exercise

Review your current professional contacts and identify the difference between people you have relationships with versus people who are just names in your database. Think about someone in your network who has genuinely helped you, then consider how you could help them or someone they know. Reach out to that person not to ask for anything, but to see how their business is going and whether there's anything you can do to support their success.

Chapter 3: Know, Like and Trust

The last time you got a cold call from someone trying to sell you something, how motivated were you to buy? Did you even want to continue the conversation, or did you hang up as fast as possible?

When someone cold calls you, they're facing a basic problem. You don't know who they are, have no reason to trust them, and probably don't like being interrupted by a stranger trying to sell you something.

Therefore, cold calling has terrible success rates. The caller starts at zero with three strikes against them. They're unknown, unliked, and untrusted. Not exactly a sound foundation for building business relationships.

Networking works on the opposite principle. Instead of trying to sell to strangers, you focus on getting people to know, like, and trust you long before you need anything from them.

"To be successful, you have to be able to relate to people; they have to be satisfied with your personality to be able to do business with you and to build a relationship with mutual trust." – George Ross

---

I discovered this principle through a vendor relationship at Trader Joe's. As Director of Computer Operations, I had authority to spend several million dollars a year on hardware and software. This made me very popular with computer salespeople. Some days it felt like every vendor in the industry wanted to pitch me their latest product.

Most of these salespeople followed the cold-call approach. They'd call or email out of nowhere, give me a brief introduction, and hurry to their main point.

Could they talk to me about purchasing their product?

Could they send me information?

Could they set up a meeting to show their software?

I didn't know these people, had no reason to trust them, and didn't like being treated as just another name on their prospect list. These calls rarely went anywhere.

But one vendor took a completely different approach. Jimmy, one of my colleagues, introduced me to Tim, a senior salesperson from a major computer reseller. The introduction was important because I trusted Jimmy's judgment. If Jimmy vouched for someone, that person immediately had credibility with me.

Tim arrived precisely on time for our lunch meeting, which was crucial. Being late to a first meeting tells me you can't be trusted with simple commitments. How can I trust you with complex business relationships if you can't manage to show up when you said you would?

He brought one of his engineers, Rusty, which showed he was serious about understanding our technical needs rather than just making a quick sale. We spent two hours discussing the computer industry, new technology trends, and the challenges we were facing with our current systems.

Here's what Tim didn't do during that lunch. He didn't try to sell me anything. He didn't pitch his products or hint that he wanted our business. Instead, he listened to our problems, asked thoughtful questions, and took detailed notes about our situation.

By the end of lunch, Tim had accomplished something remarkable. I knew who he was and what his company could do. I liked him because he'd shown genuine interest in our challenges rather than just trying to make a sale. And I was beginning to trust him because he'd demonstrated professionalism, competence, and respect for our time.

A few months later, I put out a request for proposal to several vendors for new computer systems. Tim was included on the list. After reviewing our requirements and doing his analysis, Tim declined to bid.

His reason surprised me. He felt that his company couldn't provide the best return on investment for this project. Instead, he recommended a different vendor who he believed could give us a better solution at a lower cost.

At that moment, Tim earned my complete trust. He had sacrificed a potentially large sale to do what was right for our company. He proved that his primary concern was our success, not his commission.

From that point forward, Tim became our preferred vendor for computer equipment. Not the only vendor we used, but the first one we called when we needed something. Other salespeople came and went, but Tim remained at the top of our list because I knew him, liked him, and trusted him completely.

This is the power of the know, like, and trust principle. Business relationships depend on credibility and mutual respect. Everything else is secondary.

Think about your own purchasing decisions. Do you buy from people you don't know? If you don't like someone, do you still give them your money? If you don't trust somebody, would you hand over payment before receiving their product or service?

The answer is obvious, but most business owners ignore this reality when they're trying to build their own networks. They focus on features, benefits, pricing, and competitive advantages while ignoring the fundamental human element that drives all business decisions.

Getting people to know you requires consistent visibility and communication. You can't build relationships with people who don't know you exist. This means showing up at industry events, participating in professional associations, maintaining an active presence on relevant social media platforms, and staying in regular contact with people in your network.

Getting people to like you is about showing genuine interest in their success and treating them with respect. People like people who listen to them, remember details about their lives and businesses, and look for ways to help them achieve their goals. They don't like people who only contact them when they need something or who treat every conversation as a sales opportunity.

Getting people to trust you means being consistent in your words and actions. Trust is built through keeping commitments, following through on promises, and showing integrity even when it costs you something. Tim earned my trust by recommending a competitor when it was in our best interest, even though it meant losing a sale.

When people know, like, and trust you, they naturally want to help you succeed. They refer opportunities to you, recommend you to their contacts, and give you the benefit of the doubt when problems arise.

This differs completely from transactional business relationships based on price, convenience, or features. Those relationships are fragile and temporary. As soon as someone offers a better price or more convenient service, your customers disappear.

Relationships based on know, like, and trust are much stronger. Even when competitors offer lower prices or better features, your network sticks with you because they value the relationship more than they value saving a few dollars or getting additional features they don't really need.

Building know, like, and trust takes time and can't be rushed. You can't create instant credibility with a clever marketing campaign or a persuasive sales pitch. You build it through consistent actions that show your character, competence, and commitment to other people's success.

This explains why networking is a long-term strategy, not a quick fix. The relationships you build today might not produce immediate results, but they create a foundation of trust that will support your business for years to come.

By prioritizing getting people to know, like, and trust you, sales become much easier. Instead of convincing strangers to buy from you, you're working with people who already believe in you and want to see you succeed. Instead of overcoming objections and resistance, you're collaborating with trusted partners to solve problems and create value.

This approach also makes business more enjoyable. Instead of dreading sales calls and networking events, you look forward to connecting with people you genuinely care about. Instead of feeling like you're bothering people with your outreach, you're adding value to their lives and businesses.

The know, like, and trust principle applies to every aspect of networking, whether you're meeting people online or offline, building relationships with customers, vendors, partners, or peers. It's the foundation that makes all other networking strategies effective.

Master this principle, and you'll find that building a successful business becomes much easier than you ever imagined.

Recap

People do business with people they know, like, and trust. Getting people to know you requires consistent visibility and communication. Getting them to like you means showing genuine interest in their success and treating them with respect. Gaining their trust requires consistency between your words and actions. Relationships based on know, like, and trust are stronger and more durable than transactional relationships based on price or features.

Exercise

Think about a recent significant purchase you made, either personal or business. Trace back the process that led to your decision. Did you buy from someone you knew, liked, and trusted, or was it purely a transactional decision based on price and features? Consider how you can apply the know, like, and trust principle to your own networking efforts by identifying specific actions you can take to increase your visibility, demonstrate a genuine interest in others, and build trust through consistent follow-through on commitments.

Chapter 4: Networking Is Not Sales

When you're networking, one of the biggest missteps you can make is trying to sell to people. I know that sounds backward because, obviously, the reason most people network is to grow their business and make more money.

But here's the problem. If you show up at networking events trying to sell your products or services, you're doing it wrong. And you're probably annoying everyone you meet.

Let me tell you about Dave, a guy I worked with who completely missed this point. We went to a computer convention together, and watching him operate was like witnessing a masterclass in how not to network.

The first person Dave met was Daphne, a development manager at another consulting company. Dave spent the next fifteen minutes telling her all about himself. How great he was, what amazing projects he'd worked on, how impressive his technical skills were, and why she should hire his company for her next project.

Poor Daphne barely got a word in. She kept looking over at me as if I was supposed to rescue her from this one-sided sales pitch. Dave was so busy talking about himself that he never bothered to learn anything about Daphne, her company, or what challenges she was facing.

Dave repeated this performance with every person he met. He'd launch into his elevator pitch, list his qualifications, and try to close a sale with someone he'd just met thirty seconds earlier.

Not surprisingly, Dave never heard from any of these people. He added a ton of contacts but generated zero business from the entire convention.

My approach was completely different. When I met someone like Seymour, a technical person manning a vendor booth, I focused on learning about him.

What was his role at the company?

What kinds of challenges was he dealing with?

What was he hoping to accomplish at the convention?

I asked questions and listened to the answers. I took notes on the back of his business card so I could remember details about our conversation. When I helped him, either with information or connections, I helped without expecting anything in return.

After the convention, I followed up with Seymour and everyone else I'd met, not to pitch my services but to continue the relationship. I sent useful articles, made introductions to people who might help them, and stayed in touch regularly.

Two weeks later, Seymour called me. He needed a technical manual that was out of print. He remembered our conversation and wondered if I had a copy he could borrow. I mailed him one the next day, and we stayed in contact for years afterward.

When I eventually needed to find a new job, Seymour gave me several excellent referrals that led to interviews. Dave's business cards went straight into the trash, but my relationship with Seymour created real value for both of us.

This is the fundamental difference between networking and sales. Sales is about convincing someone to buy something right now. Networking is about building relationships.

When you're selling, you're focused on your products, your services, your needs, and your goals. When you're networking, you're focused on the other person. What are their challenges? How can you help them? What resources or connections might benefit them?

"Networking is marketing. Marketing yourself, marketing your uniqueness, marketing what you stand for." – Christine Comaford-Lynch

---

The irony is that when you stop trying to sell people and start trying to help them; you end up with more sales. But those sales come through referrals, recommendations, and relationships rather than through direct pitches and high-pressure tactics.

Think about it this way. If you went to a networking meeting and asked how many people in the room were there to sell something, almost everyone would raise their hand. But if you asked how many were there to buy something, you'd see very few hands.

There's a fundamental mismatch between what people are trying to do at networking events and what happens there. Everyone's trying to sell, but nobody's trying to buy. No wonder most networking feels forced and unproductive.

The solution is to approach networking as relationship building rather than lead generation. Instead of asking, "How can I sell to this person?" ask, "How can I help this person?" Instead of thinking, "What can I get from this relationship?" think, "What can I give to this relationship?" - Haleh Houshim

---

Her philosophy: "I think that we need to have fun and play, because when you have fun, and when you're doing what you're passionate about, you can financially also create the revenue you want"

This shift in mindset changes everything about how you network. Rather than delivering elevator pitches, you ask thoughtful questions. Instead of talking about yourself, you learn about others. Instead of trying to impress people with your credentials, you show your value by being helpful and generous.

When you network this way, people see you as a resource rather than a pest. They look forward to talking with you because they know you're genuinely interested in their success. They refer opportunities to you because they trust your character and competence.

This became clear when I observed my boss Steve operate. While I was focused on technical problems, Steve was building relationships with people throughout the industry. When we faced our worst crisis, Steve's network came through for us in ways that no amount of money could have bought.

Steve never tried to sell anything to these people. He built genuine friendships based on mutual respect and shared interests. When he needed help, they were eager to provide it because they knew he would do the same for them.

It's important to clarify that this doesn't mean you never talk about your business or mention your services. Of course you do. But you do it in the context of helping others understand how you might be able to assist them, not in the context of trying to make an immediate sale.

The goal is to plant seeds that might grow into opportunities later. You want people to remember you when they hear about a job opening, a project that needs your skills, or a problem you could solve. You want them to think of you as someone who could add value to their organization or their network.

This technique depends on patience and a longer view. You might meet someone today who doesn't need your services for two years. In fact, they may never need or buy anything from you. But if you've built a genuine relationship and stayed in touch, they'll think of you when that need finally arises.

The people who are most successful at networking understand this principle. They invest time in relationships without keeping score or expecting immediate returns. They help others achieve their goals and trust that good things will come back to them in the long term.

Referrals from your network are usually higher-quality leads than anything you can generate through advertising or cold calling. People who are referred to you already have some level of trust because someone they know vouched for you.

Plus, working with referrals is more enjoyable. Instead of convincing skeptical strangers to buy from you, you're working with people who already believe you can help them. The sales process is shorter, the relationships are better, and the results are more satisfying.

So, the next time you're at a networking event, resist the urge to pitch your products or services. Focus on meeting interesting people and learning about their business. Look for ways to help them succeed. Build genuine relationships based on mutual value and respect.

You'll find that this approach not only generates better business results but also makes networking much more enjoyable and rewarding.

Recap

Networking is about developing professional connections, not making sales. Focus on learning about other people rather than talking about yourself. Ask how you can help others instead of thinking about what you can get from them. Plant seeds for future opportunities rather than trying to close deals immediately. Referrals from genuine relationships are higher quality and more enjoyable to work with than leads generated through direct sales tactics.

Exercise

Attend a networking event or have a conversation with a professional contact and practice the no-sales approach. Focus entirely on learning about the other person's business, challenges, and goals. Look for ways you might be able to help them, whether through information, connections, or resources. Notice how this changes the dynamic of the conversation and how the other person responds to your genuine interest in their success rather than your desire to sell them something.

Chapter 5: How Can I Help?

I drove over 100 miles to a job interview in Camarillo based on a five-minute phone conversation with Alasdair, the software manager at BIF AccuTell. That was a long way to drive for such a brief phone screening, but I was determined to find a new position fast.

Just a few days before, I had decided to look for another job and now had over a dozen interviews lined up, including one up in Seattle. It was a busy time, but I was motivated to move on quickly.

The reason I could line up so many interviews in such a short time wasn't that I was some hotshot programmer or that the job market was good. It was because I had spent years building a network of contacts by consistently offering help to other people in the industry.

For years, I kept in touch with people via email, phone calls, and in-person meetings. The idea was simple: stay in contact, find out how they were doing, and ask if there was anything I could do to help them out.

Usually they didn't need anything, but occasionally someone would reply that they were looking for a consultant with a certain skill, a new employee, some technical documentation, or a reference for a job they were pursuing.

Wherever possible, I gave them what help they needed without asking for anything in return. Sometimes I could help them directly, but more often I passed along a reference to somebody who could give them what they needed.

"Always give without remembering and receive without forgetting." – William Barkley

---

For example, one day I got a call asking for help. Their computer had crashed, and the data was destroyed. If they couldn't restore that information, they would be out of business. I sent over a technician right away, and he recovered their information by the end of the day. To them it was magic, although we did that kind of thing all the time.

After deciding to find a new job, the first thing I did was open my contact list and start reaching out to people in my network. I wasn't asking them for jobs. I was letting them know I was looking and asking if they knew of any companies that might hire someone with my skills.

The outcome proved incredible. No one had any positions available, but they each gave me the names of other companies that might help. More importantly, they made calls on my behalf to introduce me to the right people.

When you're looking for a job the traditional way by sending in your resume and hoping it gets picked from thousands of others, it can take months or years to find the right opportunity. You're competing against everyone else who's applying for the same position.

The advantage of using a network to hunt for a job is that you go through the back door. Either you get connected directly to the person who makes hiring decisions, or you get introduced to someone who can make that connection for you.

I lined up a dozen interviews in a matter of days because each of those managers received a personal reference about me from someone they trusted, someone in my network.

Most people enjoy being helped. Life is tough, and there are many obstacles to success. In business, the major barriers are skills, time, and knowledge. If you can provide those things for people, you become highly respected and sought after.

The fastest way to build a strong network is to communicate regularly and offer help whenever you can. Either provide the help personally or give them a reference to someone who can assist them.

Helping other people builds the foundation and solidifies the bonds between you and the people in your network. Anyone can talk, and everyone is always asking for or demanding things. But the most powerful people, the ones who can be trusted and who are competent, help others and give regularly.

Being willing to help and give, as opposed to asking and demanding, is what puts your network into overdrive. Conversely, continually asking for things, demanding help, and trying to sell is a great way to sabotage your ability to network with others.

That long drive to Camarillo paid off. A few days after the interview, Alasdair offered me a job as a Senior Designer, which I accepted. I was offered a second job as Vice President of Consulting in North Long Beach on weekends for a small startup company, which I also accepted.

The true power of networking is giving and offering help to others. When you make this your primary focus, opportunities naturally come your way because people want to help those who have helped them.

But here's the crucial point: you can't keep score. You can't help someone today and expect them to help you tomorrow. That's not how it works. The person you help might never help you directly. But their friend might. Or their colleague. Or someone they meet at a conference next year.

Networking creates a web of relationships where good deeds flow in all directions. When you consistently help others, the goodwill spreads throughout your network. People think of you as someone who adds value rather than someone who just takes from others.

This is why networking based on helping others is so much more powerful than networking based on self-promotion. When you're known as someone who helps people solve problems, people naturally want to connect with you. They see you as a resource and an asset to their own network.

When you're known as someone who's always pushing your own agenda, people avoid you. They see you as a drain on their time and energy. They might be polite when you approach them, but they won't go out of their way to help you when you need it.

The mindset shift from "What can I get?" to "What can I give?" transforms everything about how people perceive you and how they respond to your networking efforts. Instead of being seen as another person with their hand always out, you become someone people are eager to know and work with.

This approach requires patience. You might help dozens of people before receiving any direct benefit. You might give advice, make introductions, and share resources for months or years before anyone returns the favor.

But when you need help, when you're looking for a job or facing a crisis or trying to solve a problem you can't handle alone, that network of people you've helped will be there for you. They'll make calls, provide references, share opportunities, and assist you because they know you would do the same for them.

The people who understand this principle build networks that serve them throughout their entire careers. They never have to worry about finding their next job or their next customer because their network is constantly generating opportunities for them.

Those who focus on what they can get from networking struggle to build lasting relationships. They might make some short-term connections, but they don't create the deep, trusting relationships that provide real value when it matters most.

Make helping others the cornerstone of your networking strategy, and you'll discover that building a successful business and advancing your career becomes much easier than you imagined.

Recap

The most effective networking strategy is consistently helping others without expecting immediate returns. Help people solve problems, make connections, and achieve their goals. This builds strong relationships and creates goodwill throughout your network. When you need help, the people you've assisted will naturally want to return the favor. Focus on what you can give rather than what you can get, and opportunities will flow to you naturally.

Exercise

Reach out to three people in your professional network this week with the sole purpose of offering help. Ask how their business is going and whether there's anything you can do to assist them. This might be sharing an article, making an introduction, providing advice, or simply listening to their challenges. Don't ask for anything in return. Notice how these conversations differ from typical networking interactions and observe how people respond to your genuine offer of help.

Chapter 6: It's Not About You

The fastest way to kill your networking effectiveness is to make everything about you. Your problems, your needs, your goals, your services, your accomplishments, your opinions. Most people approach networking like a giant therapy session where they get to talk about themselves to anyone who will listen.

This self-centered approach destroys relationships before they start.

Nobody cares about your problems as much as you do.

Nobody is as interested in your business as you are.

Nobody wants to hear about your latest achievements unless they ask.

I learned this lesson by watching myself fail repeatedly at early networking attempts. I'd meet someone and immediately launch into my background, my expertise, my company's services, and what I was hoping to accomplish. I was so focused on presenting myself that I never learned anything about the other person.

The conversations felt forced and one-sided because they were. I used other people as an audience for my personal monologue rather than trying to understand their situations and help them succeed.

The breakthrough came when I shifted my focus from talking about myself to learning about others. Instead of preparing elevator pitches about my qualifications, I prepared questions about their businesses. Instead of listing my accomplishments, I asked about their challenges.

"You can make more friends in two months by becoming interested in other people, than you can in two years by trying to get other people interested in you." – Dale Carnegie

---

What happened next was immediate and dramatic. People became more engaged in conversations, more responsive to follow-up, and more likely to refer opportunities to me. When you prioritize others instead of yourself, they naturally become more interested in you.

This isn't manipulation or a clever networking trick. Its human nature. People like people who show a genuine interest in their lives and businesses. They avoid people who care only about themselves.

The networking conversations that lead to lasting relationships start with understanding the other person's situation.

What challenges are they facing?

What goals are they trying to achieve?

What obstacles are preventing their success?

These questions require you to listen more than you talk. Most people are terrible listeners because they're too busy thinking about what they want to say next. They treat conversations like competitions where the goal is to get their points across rather than understand what the other person needs.

I started taking notes during networking conversations, either mentally or literally, about what people told me. This forced me to pay attention to their words instead of planning my next comment. The notes also helped me remember important details for follow-up conversations.

When someone tells you they're struggling with cash flow, looking for new marketing channels, or dealing with difficult employees, they're giving you valuable information about how you might be able to help them. Most people ignore these opportunities because they're too focused on their own agenda.

The "How can I help?" mindset transforms networking from a selfish activity into a generous one. Instead of thinking about what you can get from each person you meet, you think about what you can give to them.

This might be advice based on your experience, an introduction to someone who could solve their problem, a resource that addresses their challenge, or simply a sympathetic ear when they need to talk through a difficult situation.

The help doesn't need to be huge or expensive. Sometimes the most valuable assistance is a five-minute conversation that helps someone think through a problem differently or a simple introduction that connects them with exactly the right resource.

I built some of my strongest professional relationships by helping people with minor problems that were easy for me to solve but difficult for them to handle alone. A quick technical consultation, a referral to a trusted vendor, or an introduction to a potential client created lasting goodwill.

The compound effect of helping others is remarkable. When you consistently provide value to people in your network, they start thinking of you as a resource and recommending you to others who face similar challenges.

This reputation spreads throughout your professional community. People begin reaching out to you for advice, referrals, and collaboration opportunities. Instead of chasing networking opportunities, they come to you naturally.

The mistake most people make is expecting immediate reciprocity when they help someone. They provide assistance and then wait for the other person to return the favor. When it doesn't happen immediately, they feel taken advantage of and stop helping.

This transactional approach misses the point completely. You help people because it's the right thing to do and because it builds long-term relationships, not because you expect immediate returns.

The returns come, but often from unexpected sources and in unexpected ways. The person you help today might not help you directly, but they might mention your name to someone who can provide exactly the opportunity you need.

Your networking conversations should focus primarily on understanding and helping the other person. If they ask about your business or situation, answer honestly but keep the focus on them. They'll learn what they need to know about you through your questions, your insights, and your willingness to help.

This approach requires confidence and patience. You need to trust that showing your value through helpfulness is more effective than promoting yourself through self-presentation. You need patience to build relationships gradually rather than trying to extract immediate value.

Most people struggle with this because they feel like they're not getting their message across if they don't talk about themselves extensively. They worry people won't understand what they do or how they could be helpful.

But the opposite is true. When you aim to help others, they learn much more about your capabilities, character, and value than they would from listening to your sales pitch. Your actions show your competence better than your words ever could.

The "not about you" principle applies to every aspect of networking.

Your LinkedIn posts should provide value to your network rather than promoting your achievements.

Your networking emails should offer help rather than asking for favors.

Your conference conversations should focus on learning rather than teaching.

This doesn't mean you should never talk about your business or share your expertise. It means you should do these things in the context of helping others rather than promoting yourself.

When someone asks how you achieved a particular result, share the information generously.

When someone faces a challenge you've solved before, offer specific advice.

When someone needs a service you provide, explain how you work and why you might be helpful.

But lead with their needs, not your offerings. Start with understanding their situation, then explain how your experience or services might address their specific challenges.

The professionals who master this principle become known as connectors, problem solvers, and valuable resources in their industries. People seek them out because they know these professionals will listen, understand their situations, and look for ways to help.

This reputation opens doors that no amount of self-promotion could create. When you're known as someone who helps others succeed, opportunities naturally flow to you because people want to support and work with generous, helpful professionals.

Make your networking about them, not you. Focus on understanding their challenges and finding ways to help them succeed. Your own success will follow naturally from the relationships you build through genuine service to others.

Recap

Effective networking focuses on understanding and helping others rather than promoting yourself. Lead conversations with questions about their challenges and goals instead of talking about your background and services. Listen more than you talk and look for ways to provide value through advice, introductions, or resources. Help others without expecting immediate reciprocity. Your expertise and value become apparent through your helpfulness rather than your self-promotion. This approach builds stronger relationships and creates a reputation that attracts opportunities naturally.

Exercise

For the next two weeks, approach every networking conversation with the goal of learning about the other person's challenges and finding at least one way to help them. Ask questions about their business situation, listen carefully to their responses, and offer help through advice, introductions, or resources. Track how this approach affects the quality of your networking conversations and whether people become more responsive and engaged when you focus on their needs rather than your own.

Chapter 7: Act Professional

The fundamentals of professional behavior aren't complicated, but many people get them wrong. They show up late, dress inappropriately, forget to bring basic materials, or let their emotions control the conversation.

Your appearance and demeanor either help or hurt your networking efforts. There's no neutral ground. People form impressions within seconds of meeting you, and those first impressions are difficult to change.

Being late to a networking meeting tells people you can't manage your time or keep commitments. If you can't show up when you say you will, why would anyone trust you with important business matters? Always arrive on time, preferably a few minutes early.

Your handshake matters. A weak, limp handshake suggests you lack confidence or authority. An overly aggressive handshake makes you seem like you're trying too hard to dominate the situation. Give firm, confident handshakes that match the other person's grip strength.

Eye contact shows confidence and engagement. Looking around the room while someone is talking to you suggests you're bored or looking for someone more important to talk to. Focus on the person in front of you and give them your full attention.

Dress appropriately for the situation and the people you're meeting. This doesn't always mean wearing a suit, but it does mean looking like you belong in the room. If you're not sure what's appropriate, ask someone who knows the group or error on the side of being slightly overdressed rather than underdressed.

Grooming is nonnegotiable. Clean hair, trimmed nails, fresh breath, and good hygiene are basic requirements. Avoid strong fragrances.

Come prepared with the basic tools you need to be effective. Bring something to write with and write on, business cards to exchange, and any materials that might apply to the conversation. Having these items readily available shows you're organized and taking the interaction seriously.

"Believe passionately in what you do, and never knowingly compromise your standards and values. Act like a true professional, aiming for true excellence, and the money will follow." – David Maister

---

Control your emotions during networking situations. Save your frustrations, complaints, and personal problems for your friends and family. Networking conversations should focus on business topics and positive interactions. Nobody wants to hear about your bad days or your problems with other people.

Keep the conversation professional but not stiff. You want to be friendly and approachable while maintaining appropriate boundaries. Share information about your work and interests but avoid overly personal topics or controversial subjects that might create conflict, especially politics.

Listen more than you talk and ask thoughtful questions about the other person's business and interests. Show genuine interest in their challenges and accomplishments.

Follow through on any commitments you make during networking conversations. If you promise to send information, make an introduction, or follow up on a topic, do it promptly. Your reliability in small matters shows how you'll handle larger responsibilities.

Professional behavior extends to your online presence as well. Your social media profiles, email signature, and any other digital touchpoints should reflect the same level of professionalism you show in person. Potential networking contacts often research people online before or after meeting them.

You want people to remember you as someone who was prepared, professional, and genuinely interested in building a mutually beneficial relationship. You don't want to be remembered as the person who showed up late, was poorly dressed, or dominated the conversation with inappropriate topics.

Professional behavior isn't about being fake or putting on an act. It's about showing respect to the people you're meeting and for the networking opportunity itself. When you show professionalism consistently, people are more likely to trust you, refer opportunities to you, and want to maintain a relationship with you.

The business world is full of people who have good ideas, useful skills, and valuable experience. The ones who advance their careers and build successful businesses are usually those who combine competence with professional behavior. They understand that how you present yourself is just as important as what you offer.

Master the fundamentals of professional behavior, and you'll find that people are more receptive to your networking efforts and more likely to think of you when opportunities arise.

Recap

Professional behavior in networking situations includes arriving on time, dressing appropriately, maintaining good eye contact, giving firm handshakes, and coming prepared with necessary materials. Control your emotions and keep conversations focused on business topics rather than personal problems. Listen more than you talk and follow through on commitments. Your appearance and demeanor create lasting first impressions that either help or hurt your networking effectiveness.

Exercise

Before your next networking event or professional meeting, prepare a checklist of professional behaviors to practice. Include items like arriving ten minutes early, bringing business cards and note-taking materials, preparing thoughtful questions about the other person's work, and planning appropriate attire for the situation. After the event, evaluate how well you executed these professional behaviors and identify areas for improvement in future networking situations.

Chapter 8: Strategic Networking

Most people network randomly. They meet whoever is at the next table, connect with anyone who sends them a LinkedIn request, and hope something good comes from their scattered efforts.

This is networking like throwing darts blindfolded. You might hit something, but it's probably not what you were aiming for.

Strategic networking is different. You identify the specific people who can most impact your business or career, then you figure out how to connect with them systematically.

When I was at Trader Joe's, I realized that randomly networking with everyone in the computer industry wasn't getting me anywhere. I needed to be more deliberate about who I was building relationships with.

I made a list of the twenty most influential people in my field. Not the most famous people, but the ones who made decisions that affected my work. The CTOs at major retailers. The partners at consulting firms that worked with companies like ours. The executives at software companies whose products we might use.

These weren't people I could just call up and ask to lunch. They were busy, important, and probably got dozens of similar requests every week. I needed a strategy to get their attention and build genuine relationships with them.

The crucial factor involves finding the right introduction path. Instead of trying to reach these people directly, I mapped out who they already knew and trusted.

Who were their colleagues, advisors, and business partners?

Who had worked with them before?

Who moved in their professional circles?

Once I identified these connection points, I focused on building relationships with those people first. Not because I was using them to get to someone else, but because they were valuable contacts in their own right.

This led to the CTO of a major retail chain. Direct outreach would have been ignored. But I discovered that one of my existing contacts, a consultant named Mike, had done several projects for that company. Mike knew the CTO personally and respected his work.

I spent six months deepening my relationship with Mike. We had lunch regularly; I referred business opportunities to him, and I helped him with technical challenges when I could. This wasn't manipulation. Mike and I struck up a genuine business friendship, and I enjoyed working with him.

"What I do on my networking is I make sure that I handpicked attendees globally. And if anyone...that I fit is not aligned in our networking group, I tell them nicely, don't attend" - Haleh Houshim

---

When the right moment came up naturally in conversation, I mentioned my interest in learning from other retail CTOs about how they were handling certain technology challenges. Mike immediately suggested my meeting his contact. He made the introduction, and what could have been a cold outreach became a warm referral.

That connection led to a two-hour conversation with the CTO about the future of retail technology, several follow-up discussions, and eventually a consulting opportunity when they needed expertise in an area where I specialized.

Strategic networking requires patience and planning. You can't rush it or force it. Build genuine relationships with people who can introduce you to the people you want to meet. This often means going two or three levels deep before you reach your ultimate target.

The process looks like this: identify your targets, map their networks, build relationships with people in those networks, and wait for natural opportunities to be introduced.

This approach works because it's based on trust rather than self-promotion. When someone you know and trust introduces you to someone else, that introduction carries weight. You're not a stranger trying to sell something. You're a friend of a friend with a legitimate reason to connect.

Industry conferences are goldmines for strategic networking if you approach them correctly. Most people wander around randomly, attending whatever sessions sound interesting and talking to whoever they bump into.

I'd research the speaker list and attendee roster weeks before the conference. I'd identify the five or ten people I most wanted to meet and figure out which sessions they were speaking at or attending. Then I'd plan my schedule around connecting with those specific people.

I wouldn't try to pitch them or sell them anything. I'd ask thoughtful questions about their presentation, share relevant insights from my experience, and look for ways to be helpful. The goal was to start a conversation that would continue after the conference ended.

One technique that worked well was arriving early at sessions where my target contacts were speaking. I'd sit in the front few rows and ask a thoughtful question during the Q&A period. This positioned me as someone who was engaged with their ideas and gave them a reason to remember me when I approached them afterwards.

Another strategy was hosting dinners or informal gatherings during conferences. Instead of attending the official networking events where everyone was competing for attention, I'd invite six or eight interesting people to dinner at a good restaurant.

This created a more intimate setting for genuine conversations and relationship building.

Strategic networking means thinking several moves ahead, like chess. You're not just building relationships for immediate benefit. You're creating a network that will serve your long-term goals and career development.

This means connecting with people who are currently peers but might become industry leaders in five or ten years. It means creating meaningful partnerships with people who are slightly above your current level, so you have connections to grow into as your career advances.

It also means diversifying your network beyond your immediate industry. The most valuable connections often come from adjacent fields or unexpected places. A lawyer who specializes in your industry might introduce you to potential clients. An accountant who works with businesses like yours might refer opportunities. A journalist who covers your field might become a source of industry intelligence.

Strategic networking has nothing to do with using people or manipulating relationships for personal gain. It's about being intentional and thoughtful about the professional relationships you build, so that your networking efforts produce the results you're looking for.

When you network strategically, you stop wasting time on random connections that go nowhere and start cultivating business relationships that advance your business and career goals.

Recap

Strategic networking involves identifying specific people who can most impact your business or career, then systematically developing professional relationships to connect with them. Map their existing networks and build relationships with people who can introduce you. Use industry events strategically by researching attendees and speakers beforehand. Think several moves ahead and diversify your network beyond your immediate industry. Focus your networking efforts on relationships that align with your long-term goals.

Exercise

Create a list of the ten most important people you'd like to have in your network. Research their backgrounds, current roles, and professional connections. For each person, identify at least two people who might introduce you to them. Start creating meaningful partnerships with those connection points, focusing on creating genuine value rather than just looking for introductions. Plan your approach to reach these strategic contacts over the next six to twelve months.

Chapter 9: Deep Networking Techniques

Let's say you're a writer who's just finished a book about entrepreneurship, and you want Warren Buffett to write the foreword. You have no existing relationship with him, no mutual connections, and no obvious reason he should care about your book.

Most people would either give up immediately or send a cold email that gets ignored. But deep networking can get you to almost anyone if you're willing to invest the time and effort.

Here's how you systematically work your way to someone like Buffett.

First, you research everything about him. Not just the basic biography everyone knows, but his current interests, recent interviews, charitable activities, business partnerships, and personal relationships. You study his annual shareholder letters, recent speaking engagements, and the people he mentions favorably in public.

You discover that Buffett has a long-standing friendship with Bill Gates, frequently mentions his admiration for certain business leaders, and has deep relationships with executives at companies Berkshire Hathaway owns or has invested in.

Now you map his inner circle. Who are the people he trusts most?

His business partner Charlie Munger.

His son Howard Buffett who runs the family foundation.

The CEOs of Berkshire portfolio companies he speaks about frequently.

Journalists who have covered him for decades like Carol Loomis from Fortune.

These people are still too far above your level to reach directly. So, you go another layer out.

Who knows these people?

Who works with them?

Who has interviewed them or written about them?

You might discover that a particular business school professor has written extensively about Berkshire Hathaway and has interviewed several Berkshire CEOs. Or that a journalist at a regional business publication has covered Warren Buffett's Nebraska activities for twenty years and knows people in his orbit.

Now you're getting to people you might be able to reach. The business professor speaks at conferences you could attend. The journalist writes for a publication where you could contribute an article or provide expertise.

You build relationships with people at this level.

You attend the professor's presentations and ask thoughtful questions.

You pitch article ideas to the regional business publication.

You look for ways to add value to these people's work.

This process takes months or years. You're not rushing toward your ultimate goal. You're building genuine relationships with people who are interesting and valuable to know.

Eventually, you might develop enough of a relationship with the business school professor that you can mention your book project and ask for advice about how someone like Buffett evaluates foreword requests. The professor might mention that timing matters, that Buffett gets hundreds of requests, and that the ones that succeed usually come through trusted relationships.

The professor might not offer to make an introduction, but they might provide insights about how Buffett's office operates, what kinds of projects he's interested in, or suggest other approaches that might be more realistic.

Or you might discover through your journalism connections that Buffett has a specific interest in supporting young entrepreneurs from Nebraska. This gives you a different angle to consider for your book or a different audience to focus on.

You're not trying to manipulate anyone or use people as steppingstones. You're building authentic relationships with interesting people who move in the same general orbit as your target. These relationships have value independent of whether they help you reach your goal.

Sometimes the indirect approach yields better results than the direct approach would have. Maybe the business professor mentions your entrepreneurship book to a Berkshire Hathaway CEO who is looking for educational materials for their company's management training program. That connection might be more valuable than a foreword from Buffett.

Or maybe your work with the regional business publication leads to a relationship with a local entrepreneur who becomes a mentor, business partner, or major supporter of your work. The networking process often produces unexpected opportunities that are better than what you originally sought.

Deep networking requires patience for the right moment. Even if you eventually develop relationships that could theoretically lead to Buffett, you need to wait for a natural opportunity to make the connection. Pushing too hard or asking for introductions too quickly will damage the relationships you've built.

The right moment might come when Buffett announces a new initiative related to your book's topic. Or when someone in your network mentions that Buffett's office is looking for book recommendations. Or when a major news event makes your book's subject particularly relevant.

When that moment comes, you mention your project to someone in your network and ask for advice rather than immediately requesting an introduction. "I've written this book about entrepreneurship, and given Buffett's recent comments about supporting young business owners, I'm wondering if you think it might be something his office would be interested in. What would be the best way to approach this?"

This approach puts your network contact in the position of advisor rather than being asked to spend their social capital on your behalf. They can offer suggestions, insights, or possibly volunteer to make an introduction if they think it's appropriate.

The process I've described for reaching Buffett would work for connecting with almost any high-profile person. The techniques are the same: research thoroughly, map their network, build relationships with people in their orbit, provide value consistently, and wait for the right opportunity.

The timeline might be six months for reaching a successful local business owner, two years for connecting with a Fortune 500 CEO, or five years for getting to someone like Buffett. The more powerful and busy the person, the longer the process takes and the more layers of relationships you need to navigate.

Most people aren't willing to invest this kind of time and effort, which is why most people never build relationships with truly influential people. They want shortcuts and immediate results rather than the patient, systematic approach that deep networking requires.

But if you're willing to play the long game and build genuine relationships along the way, you can eventually connect with almost anyone. The process itself often becomes more valuable than reaching your original target because of all the interesting people you meet and the opportunities that emerge along the way.

Recap

Deep networking involves systematically mapping the networks of people you want to reach and building relationships with people in their orbit. Research your targets thoroughly and identify their inner circles, then work outward to find people you can connect with. Build genuine relationships at each level rather than treating people as steppingstones. Be patient and wait for natural opportunities to emerge. The process often produces unexpected opportunities that are more valuable than your original goal.

Exercise

Choose someone influential in your industry that you'd like to connect with eventually. Research their background, current interests, and public relationships. Map out their inner circle and identify people who might know them. Then map out who might know those people. Find at least three people on the outer edge of this network that you could realistically approach. Start building relationships with those people based on genuine mutual interest rather than your ultimate networking goal.

Chapter 10: Building Your Personal Brand

Your personal brand affects every networking interaction you have, whether you're actively managing it or not. People form opinions about your competence, character, and value before they meet you based on what they've heard, read, or observed about your work.

I discovered this principle when I realized that my reputation in the computer industry was opening doors I didn't even know existed. People would agree to meetings, respond to emails, and make introductions based on what they'd heard about my work at Trader Joe's, even though I'd never met them personally.

I finally grasped that personal branding isn't about marketing yourself. It's about consistently showing your expertise and character in ways that build trust and credibility throughout your professional community.

A typical mistake is thinking personal branding is about self-promotion, social media presence, and crafting the perfect LinkedIn profile. They focus on the superficial elements while ignoring the substance that creates lasting professional reputations.

Real personal branding is about being excellent at what you do and ensuring that excellence is visible to the people who matter in your industry. It's about solving problems, helping others succeed, and building a track record of results that speaks for itself.

The foundation of any strong personal brand is competence.

You can't network your way around being bad at your job.

You can't build lasting professional relationships if you don't deliver results consistently.

You can't maintain credibility if your work doesn't meet professional standards.

In my experience, various people with impressive networking skills and polished personal brands fail because they couldn't execute when given opportunities. Their networks eventually learned that they were better at talking about work than doing it.

Conversely, I've known technically excellent professionals who struggled with networking but built strong reputations based solely on the quality of their work. Their competence became their personal brand, and people sought them out despite their poor networking skills.

The message is clear: competence comes first. Everything else is secondary.

Consistency across all professional interactions builds trust and reinforces your personal brand. This means maintaining the same level of professionalism in email communications, phone calls, meetings, and social media interactions.

People notice when your behavior varies dramatically across different situations. If you're professional in formal meetings but casual and sloppy in email communications, that inconsistency undermines your brand and creates questions about your judgment.

I learned to treat every professional interaction as a brand-building opportunity. Whether I was responding to a simple email question or presenting to senior executives, I maintained the same standards of communication and professionalism.

Industry expertise becomes a personal brand differentiator when you consistently share insights and help others understand complex topics. This doesn't require being the smartest person in the room. It requires being someone who can explain complicated subjects clearly and help others make better decisions.

I built a reputation in the computer industry by explaining technical concepts to non-technical decision makers. While other consultants focused on impressing people with their technical knowledge, I focused on helping people understand what they needed to know to make good business decisions.

This approach made me valuable to executives who needed technical guidance but didn't want to get lost in implementation details. It also distinguished me from competitors who couldn't communicate effectively outside their technical specialty.

Thought leadership through content creation amplifies your personal brand beyond your immediate network. Writing articles, speaking at conferences, and sharing insights on professional platforms establish your expertise for people who might never meet you in person.

I started writing about my industry experience after leaving Trader Joe's and discovered that content creation was one of the most effective ways to build professional credibility. People who read my articles understood my background and expertise before we ever spoke, which made networking conversations much more productive.

The key is providing genuine value rather than just promoting yourself. People share content that helps them solve problems or understand their industry better. They ignore content that's primarily about the author's accomplishments or services.

A problem-solving reputation creates one of the strongest personal brands possible. When people know you as someone who can solve troublesome problems, they think of you when those problems arise. This reputation generates networking opportunities and business referrals naturally.

I built this type of reputation by consistently helping people work through technical challenges, even when there was no immediate benefit to me. When major problems occurred in my industry, people would call me for advice because they knew I would provide useful guidance.

This problem-solving reputation became more valuable than any marketing or self-promotion I could have done. People trusted my judgment because they'd seen me help others succeed in difficult situations.

Professional integrity forms the bedrock of sustainable personal branding. This means doing what you say you'll do, admitting when you don't know something, and being honest about your capabilities and limitations.

I've watched people destroy their personal brands by over promising and under delivering, taking credit for others' work, or misrepresenting their experience and qualifications. These character issues eventually become public knowledge in professional communities, and the damage to reputation can be permanent.

Building a brand based on integrity takes longer than building one based on hype, but it creates lasting value that sustains entire careers.

Network effects multiply personal branding efforts when your reputation spreads through professional relationships. People who respect your work tell others about your expertise, creating a reputation that extends beyond your direct contacts.

This word-of-mouth branding is more powerful than any self-promotion because it comes from credible third parties who have experienced your work firsthand. When someone vouches for your competence based on their direct experience, it carries much more weight than your own claims about your abilities.

I focused on exceeding expectations for the people I worked with directly, knowing that their positive experiences would spread throughout their networks. This approach built my reputation more effectively than any marketing campaign could have.

Digital presence management has become essential for personal branding because people research others online before meeting them professionally. Your LinkedIn profile, published articles, speaking history, and social media presence all contribute to the impression people form about you.

This doesn't mean you need to be active on every platform or constantly posting content. It means ensuring that what people find when they search for you online supports the professional reputation you want to build.

I audit my digital presence regularly to ensure that search results present an accurate and professional picture of my background and expertise. This includes updating profiles, removing outdated information, and ensuring that my most relevant work is easily discoverable.

Industry recognition through awards, speaking opportunities, and media coverage validates your personal brand and provides third-party credibility. While you shouldn't chase recognition for its own sake, accepting appropriate opportunities to be recognized helps establish your reputation.

I learned to accept speaking opportunities and industry awards when they aligned with my expertise and values. These recognitions provided external validation of my competence and helped establish credibility with people who didn't know my work directly.

The key is being selective about recognition opportunities, so they enhance rather than dilute your brand. Better to be known for excellence in one area than to be mediocre across multiple areas.

Personal branding mistakes can damage your reputation and networking effectiveness. The most common errors include being inconsistent across platforms, over sharing personal information, engaging in controversial debates, and promoting yourself more than you help others.

I've seen professionals damage their brands by posting inappropriate content on social media, engaging in public arguments about non-professional topics, or promoting themselves so aggressively that they became known as self-promotional rather than helpful.

The solution is maintaining professional boundaries and remembering that everything you do professionally contributes to your brand, whether you intend it to or not.

Long-term brand building requires patience and consistent effort over years, not months. The most valuable professional reputations are built through sustained excellence and relationship building rather than short-term promotional campaigns.

I've been building my professional reputation for over three decades, and I'm still working on it. Each new project, interaction, and piece of content contributes to the overall brand I've been developing throughout my career.

The people who succeed at personal branding understand that it's not a marketing project with a completion date. It's an ongoing commitment to professional excellence that pays dividends throughout your entire career.

Your personal brand affects every networking interaction by creating expectations and perceptions before people meet you. When you build a powerful brand based on competence, integrity, and helpfulness, networking becomes much easier because people already want to connect with you.

Focus on being excellent at what you do, helping others succeed, and maintaining consistent professionalism across all interactions. The reputation you build through this approach will open networking opportunities and create business relationships that last for decades.

Recap

Personal branding affects all networking interactions by creating expectations before people meet you. Build your brand on competence, consistency, and problem-solving rather than self-promotion. Industry expertise and thought leadership establish credibility beyond your immediate network. Professional integrity forms the foundation of sustainable branding. Network effects multiply your reputation when others vouch for your work. Manage your digital presence to support your professional reputation. Focus on long-term brand building through sustained excellence rather than short-term promotional efforts.

Audit your current personal brand by searching for yourself online and reviewing your professional presence across platforms. Identify gaps between how you want to be perceived and how you currently appear to others. Choose one area where you can show expertise and begin consistently sharing valuable insights or solving problems in that space. Track how improved personal branding affects the quality of networking opportunities and relationships over the next six months.

Chapter 11: Treat Those You Network With as Partners

The single biggest mistake I see in networking is people treating other professionals like objects to be used rather than partners to be respected. They see networking contacts as buying machines, referral slot machines, or steppingstones to someone more important. This approach destroys relationships and kills networking effectiveness.

The importance of this hit me while watching myself fail repeatedly when I approached networking with a transactional mindset. I would meet people and immediately start calculating what they could do for me, how they could help my business, or whether they were worth my time based on their potential value.

This approach was obvious to everyone I met. People can sense when you're evaluating them as a resource rather than respecting them as a person. They respond accordingly by keeping their distance and avoiding deeper professional relationships.

I saw immediate improvement once I shifted my mindset from extraction to partnership. Instead of asking what people could do for me, I started asking what we could accomplish together. Instead of viewing networking as hunting for opportunities, I began seeing it as building mutually beneficial professional relationships.

The partnership mindset recognizes that every professional relationship should create value for both parties. You're not trying to get something from someone. You're exploring whether you can help each other succeed in your respective businesses and careers.

This shift in thinking transforms how you approach every networking interaction.

Instead of pitching your services, you ask about their challenges.

Instead of promoting yourself, you look for ways to help them.

Instead of trying to impress them with your accomplishments, you focus on understanding their goals.

The results are dramatically different. When people feel like you see them as partners rather than prospects, they become much more willing to share information, explore collaboration opportunities, and refer business to you.

I watched this principle in action during my years at Trader Joe's when I observed how our best vendors approached the relationship. The successful vendors didn't try to sell us products. They worked to understand our business challenges and looked for ways their solutions could help us succeed.

These vendors invested time in learning about our operations, our customers, and our goals. They brought ideas that would improve our business, not just generate sales for them. They acted as partners in our success rather than suppliers trying to extract money from us.

The result was that we gave these vendors more business, involved them in strategic planning, and maintained relationships that lasted for years. We trusted them because they had shown that they cared about our success, not just their own.

The opposite approach destroyed relationships before they started. Vendors who saw us only as a source of revenue, who pushed products we didn't need, or who tried to extract maximum profit from every interaction quickly found themselves excluded from our preferred supplier list.

When you treat people as partners, they want to work with you. When you treat them as objects to be used, they avoid you.

The partnership approach requires real interest in other people's success. You can't fake this interest or manufacture it for networking purposes. Care about helping others achieve their goals, even when there's no immediate benefit to you.

This caring attitude comes naturally when you recognize successful professionals are valuable partners, not just potential customers. They have expertise you can learn from, connections that might be helpful, and perspectives that can improve your own business thinking.

Building partnership relationships requires patience and long-term thinking. You might help someone today without seeing any return for months or years. But when opportunities arise that match your capabilities, partners think of you because they know you're invested in their success.

I've seen this principle work repeatedly in my networking efforts. The people who refer the most business to me are those I've helped with their challenges, even when there was no immediate business opportunity involved.

A consultant I helped with a technical problem five years ago still refers clients to me regularly. An entrepreneur I advised during a difficult business transition has recommended my services to dozens of other business owners. These ongoing referrals happen because I invested in their success without keeping score.

The partnership mindset also changes how you evaluate networking opportunities. Instead of focusing on what you can get from each relationship, you evaluate whether there's potential for mutual benefit and genuine collaboration.

This means you'll spend less time with people who only want to extract value from relationships and more time with professionals who understand the reciprocal nature of business partnerships.

You'll also become more selective about networking events and opportunities. Instead of trying to meet as many people as possible, you'll focus on finding professionals who share similar values about relationship building and mutual success.

The quality of your network improves dramatically when you prioritize partnership over transactional relationships. Partners provide better referrals because they understand your business well enough to identify good matches. They offer more valuable advice because they're invested in your success. They create more opportunities because they think of you when relevant situations arise.

Maintaining a partnership mindset requires constant self-examination of your motivations and approaches. It's easy to slip back into transactional thinking, especially when you're under pressure to generate business or need help with immediate challenges.

I regularly ask myself whether I'm treating networking contacts as partners or as resources to be extracted. When I catch myself calculating what someone can do for me rather than thinking about how we can help each other, I refocus on the partnership approach.

The partnership mindset also influences how you communicate about your own services and capabilities. Instead of promoting what you do, you explain how your work helps clients achieve their goals. Instead of listing your qualifications, you describe how your experience can solve problems they're facing.

This approach makes your expertise more relevant and valuable to potential partners because they can see how working with you advances their interests rather than just consuming their budget.

Partnership-based networking also requires different follow-up strategies. Instead of staying in touch to remind people about your services, you maintain contact to see how their businesses are progressing and whether you can aid.

These check-ins feel natural and welcome because they're focused on their success rather than your needs. People look forward to hearing from partners who care about their progress rather than vendors who are hunting for sales opportunities.

The partnership approach scales beautifully as your network grows. Each genuine partnership relationship enhances your ability to help others because you have more resources, connections, and expertise to offer.

Partners also amplify your networking efforts by introducing you to their networks as someone who adds value rather than extracts it. Warm introductions carry much more weight than cold outreach because they come with built-in credibility and trust.

The long-term career benefits of partnership networking extend far beyond immediate business opportunities. Partners provide strategic advice during tough decisions, offer objective perspectives on new opportunities, and can become collaborators on larger projects that neither of you could handle alone.

Some of my most successful business ventures have emerged from partnerships that started as networking relationships. What began as mutual professional respect developed into collaborative opportunities that created value for both parties.

The partnership mindset isn't about being altruistic or giving away your services for free. It's about recognizing that the most profitable long-term approach to business development is building genuine relationships with people who understand and value what you do.

When you treat networking contacts as partners, you create a professional ecosystem where everyone is invested in each other's success. This environment generates more opportunities, better referrals, and stronger business relationships than any transactional networking approach.

Stop thinking of your network as a collection of potential customers or referral sources. Start thinking of it as a community of professional partners who can help each other achieve greater success than any of you could accomplish alone.

Recap

Treating networking contacts as partners rather than objects to be used dramatically improves relationship quality and business results. The partnership mindset focuses on mutual benefit and genuine interest in others' success rather than extraction and transaction. Success with this method demands patience, long-term thinking, and authentic caring about others' goals. Partners provide better referrals, more valuable advice, and greater opportunities because they're invested in your success. The partnership approach scales effectively and creates professional ecosystems where everyone benefits from mutual support and collaboration.

Exercise

Review your recent networking interactions and honestly assess whether you approached them with a partnership or transactional mindset. Identify specific examples where you focused on what you could get versus what you could give. For your next five networking conversations, consciously adopt the partnership approach by asking about their challenges, looking for ways to help, and exploring mutual opportunities rather than promoting your services. Track how this shift affects the quality of conversations and follow-up opportunities.

Chapter 12: The Networking Meeting

The one-on-one networking meeting is the most underutilized tool in business relationship building. While everyone else wastes time at crowded mixers and conference receptions, smart networkers are having focused conversations over coffee that create lasting business relationships.

I discovered the power of individual networking meetings by accident when I started inviting people I met at events for follow-up conversations. These coffee meetings and lunch discussions produced better results than any networking event I'd ever attended.

---

*"Networking is an essential part of building wealth." –
Armstrong Williams*

The reason is simple: people can't build meaningful relationships in fifteen-minute conversations at crowded events. Real relationship building requires time, focus, and the ability to have substantive discussions about business challenges and opportunities.

Most professionals avoid individual networking meetings because they seem too formal or intimidating. They think asking someone for coffee is a bigger commitment than exchanging business cards at an event. This thinking is backwards.

A thirty-minute coffee meeting allows you to learn more about someone's business, share more about your expertise, and identify potential collaboration opportunities than a dozen brief encounters at networking events.

The networking meeting serves multiple purposes that can't be accomplished in group settings. You can have confidential discussions about business challenges, explore partnership opportunities that require detailed explanation, and build the personal trust that leads to referrals and collaboration.

I use networking meetings to deepen relationships with people I've met briefly at events, explore business opportunities that came up in casual conversations, and maintain connections with valuable contacts I haven't spoken with recently.

You're not asking for a sales meeting or trying to pitch your services. You're suggesting a conversation between professionals who might be able to help each other succeed.

The request should be specific and respectful of their time. "I'd love to hear more about the challenges you mentioned with your current marketing approach. Would you have time for a brief coffee next week to discuss it?" This approach shows genuine interest in their situation rather than pushing your own agenda.

Preparation for networking meetings requires research but shouldn't feel like cramming for an exam. Review their LinkedIn profile, recent company news, and any previous conversations you've had. Prepare thoughtful questions about their business, industry trends, and professional challenges.

The goal isn't to impress them with your knowledge but to show that you take the meeting seriously and are genuinely interested in understanding their situation.

Location choice matters for networking meetings. Coffee shops provide casual environments that encourage open conversation, but they can be noisy and distracting. Office meetings allow for more confidential discussions but might feel too formal for relationship building.

For in-person meetings, I prefer restaurants during off-peak hours or quiet hotel lobbies where we can talk without interruptions. The setting should support conversation rather than create barriers to communication.

However, the vast majority, over 90%, of my networking meetings are virtual. It's simply more convenient than trying to get together at a local establishment.

The networking meeting structure should feel natural rather than scripted, but having a mental framework helps ensure you accomplish your relationship-building goals. I typically spend the first ten minutes catching up and understanding their current situation, twenty minutes discussing their challenges and opportunities, and the final ten minutes exploring how we might help each other.

This structure allows for genuine conversation while ensuring we cover the topics that will determine whether a valuable business relationship might develop.

Starting networking meetings by asking about their business situation rather than explaining your background sets the right tone. "How's business been for you this year?" or "What's keeping you busy these days?" are natural conversation starters that focus attention on their situation.

Most people appreciate the opportunity to discuss their work with someone who's genuinely interested in understanding their challenges. This approach makes them more receptive to learning about your background and expertise.

Listening actively during networking meetings requires more discipline than listening in casual conversations. You need to understand not just what they're saying but what challenges they're facing, what opportunities they're pursuing, and how you might help them succeed.

Take notes if it feels natural, but don't let note-taking distract from the conversation. The objective is to understand their situation well enough to identify specific ways you can add value to their business.

Sharing your own background and expertise should happen naturally in response to their questions or when your experience relates to their challenges. Avoid delivering prepared presentations about your qualifications or services. Instead, share relevant stories and insights that show your competence.

When they mention a challenge you've faced before, briefly explain how you handled a similar situation. When they ask about your background, focus on experiences that relate to their current interests and needs.

Exploring mutual opportunities during networking meetings requires subtlety and genuine interest in collaboration rather than self-promotion. Look for ways your skills complement theirs, industries where your networks overlap, or challenges you've both faced that might benefit from shared solutions.

These opportunities might not be immediately obvious. The mutual benefit might be referral potential, knowledge sharing, or collaboration on future projects. The aim is to identify whether an ongoing business relationship makes sense for both parties.

Closing networking meetings appropriately sets the stage for continued relationship building. Summarize what you learned about their situation, thank them for their time, and suggest specific next steps for staying in touch.

This might be exchanging specific resources you discussed, making an introduction to someone who could help them, or scheduling a follow-up conversation about a potential collaboration opportunity.

Follow-up after networking meetings is crucial and often determines whether the relationship continues developing. Send a brief email within 24 hours thanking them for the meeting and delivering on any commitments you made during the conversation.

If you promised to send an article, make an introduction, or research a question they asked, do it immediately. Your reliability in handling these small commitments shows how you'll handle larger business relationships.

The networking meeting series approach works well for developing relationships with people who could become important business contacts. Instead of trying to accomplish everything in one conversation, plan a series of meetings that allow the relationship to develop naturally.

The first meeting focuses on understanding their situation and exploring mutual interests.

The second meeting might involve introducing them to other people in your network or discussing specific collaboration opportunities.

The third meeting could involve working together on a small project or exploring a more significant business relationship.

Virtual networking meetings have become more acceptable since the pandemic and offer advantages for busy professionals. Video calls eliminate travel time and allow for easy screen sharing when discussing projects or opportunities.

I've built valuable relationships through virtual networking meetings with people I've never met in person. The convenience factor makes people more willing to accept meeting requests, and the focused nature of video calls can improve the quality of conversation.

Networking meeting mistakes can damage relationships and waste opportunities. The most common errors include being unprepared, focusing too much on yourself, pushing for immediate business, and failing to follow through on commitments made during the meeting.

I've seen people destroy potential relationships by treating networking meetings like sales presentations or by asking for favors before establishing trust and mutual value.

The goal of networking meetings isn't closing deals or securing immediate business. It's building relationships that creates value through referrals, collaboration, knowledge sharing, and mutual support.

Some of my most valuable business relationships started with networking meetings that didn't produce immediate results but created foundations for opportunities that emerged months or years later.

Networking meetings require an investment of time and energy, but they produce better relationship-building results than any other networking activity. When you focus on individual conversations rather than trying to meet dozens of people at events, you build deeper, more valuable professional relationships.

Make networking meetings a regular part of your relationship-building strategy. The professionals who master this approach build networks of high-quality relationships that support their business goals throughout their careers.

Recap

One-on-one networking meetings build deeper relationships than group networking events by allowing focused, substantive conversations. Position meetings as professional discussions rather than sales opportunities. Prepare thoughtful questions about their business situation and challenges. Choose locations that support open conversation. Focus on understanding their needs before sharing your background. Look for genuine collaboration opportunities rather than immediate business. Follow up promptly with promised resources or introductions. Use virtual meetings when appropriate to increase convenience and participation.

Exercise

Identify five people from your recent networking activities who would benefit from individual follow-up meetings. Reach out to schedule coffee or lunch meetings positioned as professional discussions rather than sales opportunities. Prepare thoughtful questions about their business challenges and goals. During each meeting, focus primarily on understanding their situation and looking for ways to help. Track the quality of relationships developed through individual meetings compared to group networking events.

Chapter 13: Industry Events and Conferences

I used to attend conferences like a tourist. I'd show up with no plan, wander from session to session, collect business cards from vendor booths, and leave feeling like I'd learned something but accomplished nothing. I was treating conferences as entertainment instead of networking opportunities.

Everything changed when I started approaching conferences strategically. Instead of randomly attending whatever sounded interesting, I researched the attendee list if available and reviewed the speaker's information. From there, I identified the people I wanted to meet and planned my schedule around connecting with specific individuals.

The result was dramatically different. Instead of coming home with a stack of business cards from people I barely remembered, I built relationships with industry leaders who became valuable partners for years afterward.

Most people waste conferences by trying to see everything and meet everyone. They rush from session to session, attend every networking event, and exhaust themselves without building meaningful relationships. This scattershot approach produces surface-level connections that rarely turn into valuable business relationships.

Effective conference networking requires focus and preparation.

Research your target contacts thoroughly.

What are their current challenges?

What have they published recently?

What sessions are they speaking at or likely to attend?

This research helps me craft natural conversation starters and identify genuine reasons to connect.

I also research the conference schedule to identify the best networking opportunities. The official networking events are usually crowded and noisy, making meaningful conversation difficult. I look for smaller gatherings, early morning sessions, or late afternoon workshops where I'm more likely to have substantive conversations.

The biggest networking opportunities at conferences often happen outside the official schedule. I arrive a day early and stay a day late to connect with people who are doing the same. These extra days provide a more relaxed environment for relationship building without the chaos of the main conference.

The vendor exhibit area is often overlooked as a networking opportunity. While most attendees treat it like a shopping mall, I use it strategically to connect with companies and individuals in my industry. The people working vendor booths are usually decision makers or influencers who are eager to have meaningful conversations.

I avoid the mistake of trying to pitch my services to vendors. Instead, I ask thoughtful questions about their products, share insights about industry trends, and look for ways to help them succeed at the conference. This approach often leads to valuable business relationships.

Speaking at conferences is the ultimate networking accelerator. When you're a presenter, people come to you instead of you chasing them. They already know something about your expertise and have a reason to start conversations.

I started volunteering to speak at small industry events and gradually worked my way up to larger conferences. Even a brief presentation on a panel or a workshop session positions you as an expert and attracts networking opportunities.

If you can't get a speaking slot, consider hosting a hospitality suite or organizing an informal gathering. I've seen professionals host breakfast meetings, afternoon coffee sessions, or evening receptions that became the most valuable networking events at entire conferences.

You want to provide a reason for people to seek you out rather than trying to hunt them down in crowded networking events. When you create value for other attendees, they naturally want to connect with you.

Session selection should be strategic rather than educational. While learning is valuable, your primary goal at conferences should be networking. I choose sessions based on who's likely to attend rather than what I might learn.

Sessions with 50 to 100 attendees provide the best networking opportunities. Large keynote presentations are too crowded for meaningful connections. Small workshops with 15 people might not include your target contacts. Mid-sized sessions hit the sweet spot.

I arrive early to sessions and sit near the front where I can ask thoughtful questions during Q&A periods. This positions me as an engaged participant and gives speakers and other attendees a reason to remember me.

After sessions, I approach speakers with specific questions about their presentations rather than generic compliments. I also connect with other attendees who asked questions or made valuable comments during the session.

The follow-up strategy for conference networking is crucial. I email every meaningful contact within 48 hours of returning home, while the conference is still fresh in their memory. The email references our specific conversation and suggests a concrete next step for staying in touch.

Many people wait weeks to follow up or send generic messages that could have been sent to anyone. This approach wastes the momentum created by meeting in person and reduces the likelihood of building lasting relationships.

I also connect with conference contacts on LinkedIn immediately after meeting them, while I can still remember the context of our conversation. This provides a platform for ongoing interaction and keeps me visible to them between conferences.

Conference networking extends beyond the event itself. I share insights from sessions on social media, tag people I met, and continue conversations that started at the conference. This approach transforms a four-day event into months of relationship building.

The most successful conference networkers I know attend the same conferences year after year. They build relationships that deepen rather than constantly chasing new events and new contacts. Consistency creates compound networking benefits.

Travel networking opportunities often get overlooked. I've had valuable conversations with fellow conference attendees on airplanes, in airport lounges, and during shared transportation to the venue. These informal settings sometimes produce better connections than formal networking events.

Budget considerations shouldn't prevent you from attending valuable conferences. The networking ROI from the right conference can justify significant investments.

Virtual conferences require different networking strategies but can be equally effective. The chat functions and virtual meeting rooms provide opportunities to connect with attendees from around the world who would never attend in-person events.

I treat virtual conferences as seriously as in-person events. I research attendees, schedule one-on-one video calls during breaks, and follow up just as systematically. The principles remain the same even when the medium changes.

Conference networking doesn't mean collecting the most business cards or meeting the most people. It's about building genuine relationships with the right people who can help you achieve your business goals while you help them achieve theirs.

When you approach conferences strategically and focus on relationship building rather than information gathering, you'll discover that these events become powerful catalysts for business growth and career advancement.

Recap

Effective conference networking requires preparation, focus, and strategic planning rather than trying to see everything and meet everyone. Research attendees and speakers beforehand to identify target connections. Choose sessions based on networking opportunities rather than just educational content. Arrive early and stay late for better networking opportunities. Follow up within 48 hours with specific references to your conversations. Consider speaking, hosting events, or volunteering to position yourself as a resource rather than just another attendee.

Exercise

Before your next conference, research the attendee list and speaker roster to identify ten people you'd like to meet. Create a strategic plan for connecting with these individuals based on their session participation and interests. Book dinner reservations or plan informal gatherings to create networking opportunities outside the official schedule. Track your success rate in connecting with target contacts and measure the quality of relationships built compared to previous conference experiences.

Chapter 14: The Standard Networking Meeting

I showed up at my first and only BNI meeting at 6:30 in the morning expecting the worst. I'd heard about these weekly breakfast gatherings where businesspeople sit around a table, give each other referrals, and practice their elevator pitches. It sounded like my personal nightmare.

The room was full of insurance agents, real estate brokers, accountants, and small business owners clutching coffee cups and looking like they'd rather be anywhere else. Everyone had laminated business cards and practiced smiles. The energy felt forced and desperate.

As an introvert with ADHD, sitting through the structured presentations and mandatory participation was torture. The rigid format, the forced enthusiasm, the requirement to perform on cue. Everything about the meeting was designed for extroverts who thrive on group interaction and scheduled social performance.

But something unexpected happened during that meeting. I watched a plumber get three solid referrals from people who genuinely knew his work and trusted him to take care of their clients. A web designer landed a project from an accountant whose client needed a new website. An attorney got introduced to a business owner who was facing a legal issue.

Actual business was happening. Money was changing hands. Relationships were generating actual results.

That's when I understood that standard networking meetings serve a specific purpose for certain types of businesses. They're not networking in the truest sense. They're structured referral systems that can be effective if you fit the right profile.

Standard networking meetings follow a predictable format. Members arrive early for informal conversation. Someone leads a brief presentation about networking principles or business development. Each person gives a 30-second commercial describing their business and what kinds of referrals they're looking for. Then there's time for one-on-one conversations and follow-up meetings.

The most successful groups limit membership to one person per profession. Only one insurance agent, one accountant, one real estate broker. This eliminates direct competition within the group and encourages members to refer business to each other rather than keeping opportunities for themselves.

BNI is the largest and most organized of these groups, but the format appears everywhere. Chamber of Commerce breakfast meetings, industry association gatherings, and local business clubs all use variations of the same structure.

The system works brilliantly for certain types of businesses. Service providers who depend on local referrals can build steady revenue streams through consistent participation in these groups.

A tax accountant I met through BNI generated over $100,000 in new business during his first year in the group. He showed up every week, gave referrals to other members, and became known as someone who could handle complex tax situations for small businesses. Other members started referring their clients to him regularly.

An HVAC contractor built his entire business model around networking group referrals. He joined three different groups, participated consistently, and did excellent work for every referral he received. Within two years, he had more business than he could handle and was referring overflow work to other contractors.

The key factor in both cases was that these businesses served local markets with clear, immediate needs. When someone's air conditioning breaks or they need tax help, they want a referral to someone trustworthy who can solve their problem quickly.

Standard networking meetings excel at connecting people who have immediate, specific needs with service providers who can solve those problems. The regular weekly format means members learn about each other's businesses and can make informed referrals.

But this format has severe limitations for many types of businesses.

High-ticket service providers rarely succeed in standard networking meetings. If you're selling $50,000 consulting engagements or $500,000 software implementations, the small business owners at most networking meetings aren't your target market.

I watched a management consultant struggle for months in a BNI chapter, trying to explain complex organizational development concepts to people who own pizza restaurants and auto repair shops. He never received a single qualified referral because nobody in the room had any connection to companies that needed his services.

Technology businesses face similar challenges. The CTO of a startup I knew joined a Chamber of Commerce networking group hoping to find investors or strategic partners. Instead, he spent his time listening to insurance pitches and learning about carpet cleaning services. The mismatch was obvious to everyone.

Professional services that require specialized knowledge or serve niche markets don't fit the standard networking meeting model. If your ideal clients are Fortune 500 executives, venture capitalists, or specialized industry professionals, you won't find them at breakfast meetings with local business owners.

The referral-based model also breaks down when relationships matter more than transactions. Standard networking meetings assume that a good referral is primarily about matching a need with a service provider. They don't account for the complex relationship dynamics that drive high-level business decisions.

When I was buying computer systems for Trader Joe's, I didn't just need a vendor who could provide the equipment. I needed someone I trusted to understand our unique requirements, handle implementation challenges, and support our systems for years. Those relationships required much more depth than standard networking meetings could provide.

Geographic limitations also restrict the effectiveness of standard networking meetings. Most groups focus on local businesses, which works fine for restaurants, retail stores, and service businesses that serve local markets. But if your business operates nationally or internationally, local referrals have limited value.

The weekly time commitment presents another barrier for busy professionals. Standard networking meetings require consistent attendance to be effective. Missing meetings means missing referral opportunities and losing visibility within the group. This works for business owners who control their schedules but can be impossible for executives, consultants, or professionals with demanding travel requirements.

Some groups, such as BNI, may penalize you for showing up late, not attending, or not meeting the quota of referrals. One reason I never joined is I felt that after paying $1,500 for a year-long membership, they had no right to subject me to punitive actions of this nature.

The forced nature of standard networking meetings can also work against relationship building. When everyone's expected to give referrals and ask for business, the interactions feel transactional rather than authentic. People participate because they're supposed to, not because they're genuinely interested in helping each other.

I've seen many examples of standard networking meetings that turned into mutual back-scratching exercises where members referred business to each other whether or not it made sense for their clients. The focus shifted from providing value to meeting referral quotas.

Despite these limitations, standard networking meetings remain valuable for businesses that fit the model. Local service providers, retail businesses, and professionals who serve small business markets can generate significant revenue through consistent participation.

The key is understanding whether your business fits the format before investing time and money in membership. If you serve local markets, have clear referral opportunities, and can commit to regular attendance, standard networking meetings might be perfect for you.

If you sell complex services, serve specialized markets, or work with high-level decision makers, you'll probably waste your time in standard networking meetings. You need different networking strategies that connect you with your actual target market.

The mistake many people make is treating standard networking meetings as the only way to network. They join BNI or similar groups, struggle to get results, and conclude that networking doesn't work for their business. Wrong conclusion. Standard networking meetings don't work for their business. Networking absolutely can work, but they need different approaches.

Before committing to any standard networking group, observe its meetings and analyze its membership.

Do the other members serve similar markets? Can they realistically refer business to you?

Do their referral needs match what you can provide?

If the answers are no, save yourself time and membership fees.

Standard networking meetings are one tool in the networking toolbox. They're highly effective for certain businesses and completely wrong for others. Know the difference before you commit.

Recap

Standard networking meetings like BNI follow structured formats designed to generate referrals among local business owners. They work well for service providers who serve local markets with immediate, clear needs. They're ineffective for high-ticket services, specialized markets, complex B2B sales, or businesses that serve national or international clients. The weekly time commitment and transactional nature can limit their effectiveness for relationship-building. Success depends on whether your business model matches the format and membership of the specific group.

Exercise

Research three standard networking groups in your area and attend their meetings as a visitor or guest. Analyze the membership to determine whether other attendees serve your target market and whether they could realistically refer business to you. Consider whether the time commitment and meeting format align with your business goals and schedule. Decide about participation based on fit rather than the general concept of networking.

Chapter 15: Digital Networking

When I left Trader Joe's to become a writer, I thought my networking days were behind me. The computer industry ran on in-person relationships, handshakes, and face-to-face meetings. The writing world was completely different. Authors lived online, built careers through social media, and collaborated with people they'd never met.

I had to learn digital networking from scratch, and I made every mistake possible.

Initially, I treated LinkedIn like a digital business card. I'd post articles hoping people would notice, connect with random authors and editors, and wonder why nothing happened. I was networking like it was 1995 in a 2015 world.

Then, I became a senior branding expert at LinkedIn Makeover. For two years, I wrote hundreds of LinkedIn profiles for executives, entrepreneurs, ambassadors, and professionals who wanted to build their personal brands online.

This job taught me how LinkedIn works. Not the theory you read in articles, but the reality of what makes profiles successful and what creates genuine engagement on the platform.

Most people use LinkedIn wrong. They treat it like a resume repository or a place to broadcast achievements. The true power is in the conversations and relationships you build there.

Writing profiles for executives taught me that LinkedIn success isn't about having the most connections or the fanciest job title. It's about positioning yourself as someone who adds value to conversations in your field.

The best profiles I wrote weren't for the most accomplished people. They were for people who understood their audience and spoke directly to the problems those people were trying to solve.

A software consultant's profile that focused on helping companies avoid costly implementation mistakes generated more engagement than a Fortune 500 CTO's profile that just listed his impressive credentials.

This insight transformed my approach to my own digital networking. Instead of trying to impress people with my background, I focused on demonstrating value through my interactions.

"Social media is changing the way we communicate and the way we are perceived, both positively and negatively. Every time you post a photo, or update your status, you are contributing to your own digital footprint and personal brand." – Amy Jo Martin

---

I started engaging with posts by leaving thoughtful comments that added to the discussion. When someone posted about self-publishing challenges, I shared a specific insight from my experience. When editors discussed manuscript evaluation, I asked questions that revealed I understood their process.

This approach took more time than broadcasting my own content, but it was far more effective. People started recognizing my name and engaging with my posts. They began reaching out with questions, collaboration opportunities, and referrals.

My LinkedIn Makeover experience also taught me the power of strategic content creation. The profiles that generated the most opportunities weren't the ones that talked about credentials. They were the ones that addressed specific problems their target audience was facing.

I applied this to my own content strategy. Instead of writing generic posts about writing, I created content that solved specific problems for other authors. How to work with freelance editors. Common book cover design mistakes. Email list building strategies that work.

These posts attracted attention from other writers dealing with similar challenges. They commented with their own experiences, shared the articles with their networks, and reached out privately for advice. This led to actual relationships and business opportunities.

The content also attracted service providers who worked with authors. Editors, designers, and marketing consultants began following my work and reaching out when they had relevant opportunities.

Through writing LinkedIn profiles, I learned that the platform's algorithm rewards engagement over reach. A post that generates meaningful comments and discussions will be shown to more people than a post with lots of likes but no conversation.

This meant that asking thoughtful questions and creating content that sparked discussion was more valuable than sharing impressive announcements or achievements.

Email remains one of the most underutilized digital networking tools. Most people focus on social media and ignore the power of direct communication.

When I read an article by another author that provided genuine value, I would send a brief email explaining what I found useful and asking a follow-up question. Not a request for anything, just engagement with their work.

Most people were surprised to receive thoughtful feedback. Many replied with detailed responses and continued the conversation. Some of these email exchanges turned into lasting professional relationships.

Online communities became crucial to my networking strategy. I joined writing-focused Facebook groups and forums, but instead of immediately promoting my services, I spent weeks observing and learning.

I noted what questions came up repeatedly, what challenges people were facing, and who the respected voices were in each community.

Then I started participating by answering questions where I had relevant experience. When someone asked about LinkedIn profiles for authors, I shared insights from my LinkedIn Makeover work. When new writers asked about platform building, I explained strategies I'd seen work for my clients.

This established me as someone with real expertise who was willing to help. People started reaching out privately for advice. Some became clients. Others referred business to me. A few became collaborators on larger projects.

My LinkedIn Makeover experience taught me that digital networking success comes from consistency and authenticity. You can't fake expertise or manipulate your way to meaningful relationships online.

The professionals whose profiles generated the best results were those who genuinely understood their field and consistently provided value to their network. They didn't try to be everything to everyone. They focused on serving a specific audience exceptionally well.

Digital networking requires the same fundamental principles as in-person networking. Help others before asking for help. Focus on building genuine relationships rather than collecting connections. Be consistent in your efforts.

The difference is scale and speed. A single well-crafted LinkedIn post can reach hundreds or even thousands of potential networking contacts. A thoughtful comment on someone's article can introduce you to their entire network. The compound effect of consistent digital networking can dramatically expand your professional opportunities.

But the fundamentals remain the same. People do business with people they know, like, and trust. Digital platforms just give you more efficient ways to show those qualities to a larger audience.

Recap

Digital networking follows the same fundamental principles as in-person networking but operates at greater scale and speed. LinkedIn success comes from engaging meaningfully with others' content rather than just broadcasting your own. Create content that solves specific problems for your target audience. Use email for deeper relationship building. Participate genuinely in online communities before promoting yourself. Consistency and authenticity matter more than impressive credentials or large follower counts.

Exercise

Audit your current LinkedIn activity for the past month. Count how many times you posted your own content versus how many meaningful comments you left on others' posts. For the next two weeks, flip this ratio. Spend more time engaging with others' content through thoughtful comments than creating your own posts. Track the difference in response and relationship building.

Chapter 16: Virtual and Hybrid Networking

The pandemic changed networking forever. Overnight, conferences moved online, business meetings became Zoom or Skype (remember Skype?) calls, and networking events turned into awkward virtual gatherings where everyone talked over each other.

Most people treated virtual networking like a poor substitute for the real thing. They waited for things to get back to normal so they could return to handshakes and business cards.

"If we all work together there is no telling how we can change the world through the impact of promoting positivity online."
– Germany Kent

I saw it differently. Virtual networking isn't inferior to in-person networking. It's a different tool with its own advantages and techniques.

When conferences first moved online in 2020, I watched hundreds of people struggle with the format. They'd sit passively through presentations, rarely unmute themselves to ask questions, and disappear immediately when sessions ended.

I took a more aggressive approach. I participated actively in chat discussions, asked thoughtful questions during Q&A, and followed up directly with speakers and other attendees after sessions.

This worked better than I expected. Speakers remembered me because so few people engaged meaningfully during virtual events. Other attendees reached out because I'd made interesting points in the chat or asked questions they were thinking about.

Virtual events made it easier to connect with high-level people who would be surrounded by crowds at in-person conferences.

When everyone's in individual boxes on a screen, there's no VIP section or exclusive networking area. Everyone has equal access to the chat and Q&A functions.

I connected with industry leaders during virtual events who I never would have been able to approach at traditional conferences. The democratizing effect of virtual networking opened doors that had been closed in the physical world.

Virtual networking requires different strategies than in-person networking. You can't rely on physical presence, body language, or casual conversations during coffee breaks. You need to be more intentional and direct in your approach.

Chat functions became the new networking floor. Instead of wandering around looking for interesting conversations, I'd watch for thoughtful comments in the chat and reach out to those people privately during or after the session.

Many virtual platforms allow private messaging during events. I used this feature to continue conversations that started in the public chat or to reach out to people whose questions or comments showed they were dealing with similar challenges.

The follow-up became even more important in virtual networking because the connections felt less personal. I emailed everyone I'd connected with within 24 hours of a virtual event, referencing our specific conversation and suggesting ways to stay in touch.

Hybrid events present their own challenges and opportunities. These combine in-person and virtual attendance, creating two different networking experiences happening simultaneously.

I attended several hybrid conferences as a virtual participant and found that speakers often paid more attention to online questions than in-person ones. Virtual attendees had to be more thoughtful and specific in their questions, which made them stand out.

The virtual chat often became more substantive than the side conversations happening in the physical room. People felt more comfortable sharing insights and asking detailed questions when they could type them out rather than speaking in front of a crowd.

For hybrid events that I attended in person, I engaged with both the physical audience and the virtual participants. I'd reference comments from the online chat during my own questions or conversations, which helped bridge the two audiences.

Small group virtual networking requires completely different skills than large virtual events. Video calls with three to six people can be more intimate and focused than equivalent in-person meetings.

Someone needs to facilitate the discussion to avoid the awkward silence and talking-over-each-other problems that plague virtual group conversations.

I found that virtual small group meetings often produced better outcomes than in-person equivalents because people were more focused and less distracted. There were no side conversations, phone checking, or other interruptions that happen in physical meetings.

One-on-one virtual networking became my preferred method for initial relationship building. Video calls eliminate travel time and scheduling complications while still allowing for face-to-face interaction.

I could have meaningful conversations with people across the country or around the world without either of us leaving our offices. This dramatically expanded my potential networking reach and made it easier to maintain relationships with people in distant locations.

The key to successful virtual one-on-ones is treating them as seriously as in-person meetings. Good lighting, a professional background, clear audio, and a stable internet connection are non-negotiable. Technical problems destroy the relationship-building potential of virtual meetings.

Virtual networking also requires different follow-up strategies. You can't hand someone a business card or leave them with a physical reminder of your conversation. Email becomes even more critical for maintaining connections made during virtual interactions.

I developed templates for post-event follow-up emails that referenced specific aspects of our virtual conversation. This helped people remember who I was and what we'd discussed, since virtual interactions can feel less memorable than in-person meetings.

Recording capabilities in virtual meetings created new opportunities for content creation and relationship building. With permission, I recorded valuable conversations and used highlights to create content that benefited my entire network.

Virtual networking events also generated different content opportunities. I could screenshot interesting chat discussions, quote insightful comments from other participants, and create summaries of valuable sessions to share with my broader network.

The asynchronous nature of virtual networking became one of its biggest advantages. I could participate in online discussions, comment on posts, and build relationships across different time zones without coordinating schedules.

Virtual networking groups and communities began operating 24/7 rather than meeting at specific times. This made networking accessible to people with busy schedules or those in different geographic locations.

The combination of virtual and in-person networking created more powerful relationship-building opportunities than either approach alone. I could meet someone virtually, develop a relationship through online interactions, and then strengthen it through in-person meetings when opportunities arose.

Virtual networking isn't going away. Even as in-person events returned, many organizations kept virtual options because they realized the benefits of broader participation and lower barriers to entry.

The professionals who learned to network effectively in virtual environments gained a significant advantage. They could build relationships more efficiently, connect with people regardless of geographic location, and maintain networks that would be impossible to sustain through in-person meetings alone.

Virtual and hybrid networking require the same fundamental principles as traditional networking. Focus on helping others, building genuine relationships, and providing consistent value. The tools and tactics are different, but the underlying approach remains the same.

Recap

Virtual networking requires different strategies than in-person networking but offers unique advantages including democratized access to influential people and geographic flexibility. Engage actively in virtual events through chat discussions and Q&A participation. Follow up quickly after virtual interactions since they feel less memorable. Hybrid events create opportunities to bridge physical and virtual audiences. One-on-one virtual meetings can be more focused than in-person equivalents. Technical quality is crucial for virtual relationship building.

Exercise

Attend a virtual networking event or webinar this week and practice active participation. Ask at least one thoughtful question during the Q&A, make several substantive comments in the chat, and identify three people to follow up with privately after the event. Compare the quality and quantity of connections made through this active virtual approach versus passive virtual attendance at previous events.

Chapter 17: Using TikTok and Instagram for Networking

Most business professionals think TikTok and Instagram are for teenagers posting dance videos and food photos. They're wrong. These platforms have become powerful networking tools for certain types of businesses, but only if you understand how they work.

I was skeptical about social media networking until I watched a real estate agent in Phoenix build a million-dollar business almost entirely through Instagram. She wasn't posting selfies or vacation photos. She was creating content that showed her expertise, showcased properties, and built trust with potential clients.

Within two years, she had 50,000 followers and was getting five to ten serious inquiries per week from people who wanted to work with her. Her content attracted both buyers and sellers because she consistently provided valuable information about the Phoenix real estate market.

This wasn't luck or viral content. It was strategic networking through content creation.

TikTok and Instagram networking works differently than traditional networking. Instead of meeting people one-on-one at events, you're broadcasting your expertise to potentially thousands of people who share your interests or face similar challenges.

The key is understanding that these platforms reward authentic expertise over polished marketing. People can spot fake content immediately, and the algorithms punish content that feels like advertising. You need to provide genuine value if you want to build a following that translates into business opportunities.

I started experimenting with short-form content after watching several consultants and coaches build substantial businesses through these platforms. The consultants who succeeded weren't the ones with the fanciest production values. They were the ones who consistently shared practical insights that solved actual problems.

A business consultant I follow built a six-figure practice by posting daily TikTok videos answering common questions about small business operations. His content wasn't revolutionary, but it was consistently helpful. People started reaching out for more detailed advice, which led to paid consulting engagements.

The networking happens in the comments and direct messages. When you create content that resonates with your target audience, they start conversations with you. These conversations can develop into professional relationships just like any other networking interaction.

But here's where most business professionals screw this up. They treat social media as a broadcasting platform instead of a networking tool. They post content and expect people to come to them. That's not how it works.

Successful social media networking requires active engagement with other people's content. You need to comment thoughtfully on posts by people in your industry, respond to comments on your own content, and use direct messages to continue conversations that start in public.

I spent six months analyzing how successful professionals use these platforms for networking. The pattern was consistent. They spent as much time engaging with other people's content as they did creating their own. They built relationships through consistent interaction, not just content creation.

The real estate agent I mentioned didn't just post property videos. She commented on posts by mortgage brokers, interior designers, contractors, and other real estate professionals. She built a network within her industry that generated referrals and collaboration opportunities.

TikTok and Instagram are effective for service-based businesses that can show their expertise through short-form content.

Fitness trainers, consultants, designers, attorneys, accountants, and coaches have all built substantial networks through these platforms.

But the approach doesn't work for every type of business. If you're selling complex B2B services or working with high-level executives, your target audience probably isn't scrolling through TikTok looking for vendors. You need to match your networking strategy to where your audience spends time.

The content that generates the best networking results is educational rather than promotional. People follow accounts that teach them something useful, not accounts that constantly pitch products or services. The sales conversations happen privately after you've built trust through valuable content.

I learned this lesson by tracking the performance of different types of content. Posts that directly promoted my services got minimal engagement. Posts that shared practical advice or industry insights generated comments, shares, and direct messages from potential clients and collaborators.

Networking conversations often start with simple comments on your content. Someone asks a follow-up question, shares their own experience, or requests advice about a specific situation. You respond thoughtfully, and the conversation moves to direct messages where you can build a more personal connection.

These digital conversations follow the same principles as in-person networking. You focus on helping the other person, ask thoughtful questions about their business, and look for ways to add value to their work. The medium is different, but the relationship-building process is the same.

Platform choice matters for social media networking. TikTok skews younger and is better for reaching consumers and small business owners. Instagram has a broader demographic range and works well for both B2B and B2C networking. LinkedIn remains the primary platform for corporate and executive networking.

The key is understanding where your target audience spends time and what type of content they consume on each platform. A financial advisor might use TikTok to reach young professionals just starting their careers and Instagram to connect with established business owners planning for retirement.

Consistency is crucial for social media networking success. Posting occasionally when you remember won't build relationships or generate business results. The professionals who succeed post regularly and engage with their audience consistently.

But consistency doesn't mean posting multiple times per day or spending hours on social media. The real estate agent I follow posts one Instagram video per day and spends about 30 minutes responding to comments and engaging with other accounts. That consistent effort has generated millions of dollars in business.

I see that a frequent mistake business professionals make with social media networking is expecting immediate results. Building a following and generating business through these platforms takes time. You need to invest months of consistent effort before seeing significant networking results.

The professionals who quit after a few weeks because they're not getting immediate leads miss the point entirely. Social media networking is about building long-term relationships and establishing your reputation as a knowledgeable resource in your field.

Analytics help you understand what content resonates with your audience and generates networking opportunities. Track which posts generate the most comments and direct messages, not just likes and views. The posts that start conversations are the ones that build relationships.

I also track the business results from social media networking.

How many consulting inquiries came from TikTok comments?

How many referrals resulted from Instagram connections?

This data helps me understand which platforms and content types are worth my time.

Social media networking isn't a replacement for traditional networking. It's an additional tool that can expand your reach and connect you with people you'd never meet through in-person events or professional associations.

The combination can be powerful. You might meet someone through a TikTok comment thread, develop the relationship through direct messages, and eventually meet for coffee to discuss potential collaboration. The digital connection becomes the foundation of a real-world business relationship.

But social media networking requires the same authenticity and focus on helping others that makes traditional networking effective. If you approach these platforms with a sales mindset rather than a relationship-building mindset, you'll fail just as badly as people who treat in-person networking like a sales opportunity.

Use TikTok and Instagram to show your expertise, provide value to your target audience, and start conversations with potential clients and collaborators. Treat the platforms as networking tools rather than marketing channels, and you might be surprised by the business relationships you can build.

Recap

TikTok and Instagram can be effective networking tools for service-based businesses when used to show expertise rather than promote services. Success requires consistent content creation plus active engagement with other users' content. Educational content generates better networking results than promotional content. Platform choice should match your target audience. Consistency and patience are essential since social media networking takes time to produce business results. Track conversation-starting content and business outcomes rather than just vanity metrics.

Exercise

Choose either TikTok or Instagram based on where your target audience is most active. Create a content calendar for one month of educational posts related to your expertise. Post consistently and spend equal time engaging thoughtfully with content from others in your industry. Track which posts generate comments and direct messages rather than just likes and views. After 30 days, evaluate whether the conversations started through your content could develop into valuable business relationships.

Chapter 18: Networking for Introverts

The thought of working a room full of strangers made me want to hide under my desk. The standard networking advice felt like torture: attend mixer events, give elevator pitches, and make small talk with dozens of people.

This advice is wrong for introverts. We don't need to become extroverts to network effectively. We need different strategies that work with our natural tendencies rather than against them.

The breakthrough came when I realized that my best professional relationships had developed through one-on-one conversations, not group events. The consultants, vendors, and colleagues who became valuable contacts were people I'd gotten to know through individual meetings, not networking mixers.

Introverts often build deeper, more meaningful relationships than extroverts because we focus on quality over quantity. While extroverts might meet 20 people at an event, introverts might have one substantive conversation that leads to a lasting professional relationship.

What matters most is designing a networking approach that leverages these strengths instead of fighting them.

One-on-one meetings are the introvert's secret weapon for networking. Instead of trying to compete for attention in crowded rooms, I started suggesting coffee meetings, lunch conversations, and office visits with people I wanted to get to know better.

These individual meetings allow for deeper conversations about business challenges, industry trends, and professional goals. Without the distractions and energy drain of large groups, introverts can showcase their listening skills, analytical thinking, and genuine interest in helping others.

I found that busy professionals often preferred these focused meetings to networking events. They could have substantive conversations without the superficial small talk that dominates group networking situations.

Written communication gives introverts a significant advantage in networking. While extroverts might excel at spontaneous conversation, introverts often communicate more effectively through email, where they can think through their responses and craft thoughtful messages.

I started building relationships through email exchanges long before meeting people in person. This allowed me to show my expertise, ask thoughtful questions, and establish rapport without the energy drain of face-to-face interaction.

Many of my strongest professional relationships began through email conversations that eventually led to phone calls and in-person meetings. The digital relationship building created a foundation that made the eventual face-to-face meetings more comfortable and productive.

Industry expertise becomes a networking multiplier for introverts. When you're known as someone with deep knowledge in a specific area, people seek you out rather than you having to chase them at networking events.

I focused on becoming genuinely helpful to people in my industry by developing specialized knowledge and sharing insights through writing and speaking. This positioned me as a resource that people wanted to connect with, eliminating the need for aggressive networking tactics.

Content creation and thought leadership work particularly well for introverts because they allow you to share your expertise on your own schedule and in your preferred communication style. People who read your articles or attend your presentations already understand your value before meeting you.

Strategic event attendance helps introverts maximize networking results while minimizing energy drain. Instead of attending every networking opportunity, I became selective about which events deserved my time and energy.

I looked for smaller, more focused gatherings rather than large mixer events. Industry conferences with 100 to 200 attendees provided better networking opportunities than regional business events with 500 people. Workshops and educational sessions created more substantive interaction than cocktail parties.

I also learned to attend events strategically. Arriving early meant dealing with smaller crowds and having easier access to speakers and organizers. Leaving before peak attendance helped me avoid the energy drain of overcrowded rooms.

Preparation becomes crucial for introverts attending networking events. While extroverts might thrive on spontaneous interaction, introverts perform better when they have clear goals and conversation strategies.

Before attending any event, I researched the attendee list, identified specific people I wanted to meet, and prepared conversation starters based on their backgrounds and interests. This preparation reduced anxiety and increased the likelihood of meaningful connections.

I also prepared my introduction and key talking points so I wouldn't struggle with spontaneous self-presentation in group settings. Having these elements ready eliminated the mental energy required for on-the-spot creativity.

Follow-up becomes a competitive advantage for introverts because we typically prefer written communication and have more patience for evolving relationships. While extroverts might focus on immediate connection, introverts excel at nurturing relationships for the long term.

I developed systematic follow-up processes that turned brief networking encounters into ongoing relationships. Email exchanges, article sharing, and regular check-ins allowed me to build trust and show value without the pressure of constant face-to-face interaction.

Online networking platforms provide ideal environments for introverts to build professional relationships. LinkedIn, industry forums, and social media platforms allow for thoughtful engagement without the energy requirements of in-person networking.

I found I could build meaningful relationships through online interaction that eventually translated into valuable business connections. The asynchronous nature of digital communication played to my strengths while eliminating many of the challenges of real-time networking.

Small group networking offers a middle ground between one-on-one meetings and large events. Mastermind groups, peer advisory circles, and industry roundtables provide networking opportunities with manageable group sizes and structured formats.

These settings allow introverts to contribute meaningfully to group discussions without the chaos of large networking events. The regular meeting schedules also provide time to build relationships gradually rather than forcing instant connection.

Energy management becomes essential for introverts who want to network effectively. Unlike extroverts who gain energy from social interaction, introverts need to plan for the energy drain of networking activities and build in recovery time.

I learned to limit myself to one networking event per month and to schedule downtime afterward. Trying to attend multiple events in short periods led to burnout and reduced effectiveness at each interaction.

I also discovered that certain types of networking activities were less draining than others. Industry education events required less energy than pure networking mixers. One-on-one meetings were energizing rather than draining when focused on helping others solve problems.

Leveraging existing relationships helps introverts expand their networks without the stress of cold networking. Instead of meeting strangers at events, I asked colleagues and friends for introductions to people I wanted to know.

These warm introductions eliminated the awkwardness of initial contact and provided natural conversation starters. People were more receptive to relationship building when we had mutual connections and a shared context.

The referral approach also played to introvert strengths by focusing on helpful problem-solving rather than self-promotion. When I could help someone by making the right introduction, the networking felt natural and valuable rather than forced.

Hosting events or gatherings can be more effective for introverts than attending other people's events. When you're the host, people come to you rather than you having to work the room. You also control the format, guest list, and environment.

I started hosting small industry dinners and informal meetups that attracted the people I wanted to connect with. These events provided networking opportunities in settings I could manage and control, reducing anxiety while producing better relationship-building outcomes.

Digital tools help introverts manage networking relationships more systematically. CRM systems, contact management apps, and calendar reminders allow for consistent relationship maintenance without relying on memory or spontaneous outreach.

These tools particularly benefit introverts because they support planned, thoughtful communication rather than requiring constant social awareness and spontaneous relationship management.

The goal of introvert networking isn't to become an extrovert. It's about building a networking approach that works with your natural tendencies and produces genuine business results. Quality relationships matter more than quantity of contacts.

Focus on building deeper relationships with fewer people rather than trying to meet everyone at every event. Use your natural tendencies toward thoughtful communication, careful listening, and patience to create networking advantages that extroverts often struggle to achieve.

Recap

Introverts can network effectively by focusing on one-on-one meetings, written communication, and deeper relationship building rather than trying to emulate extrovert networking styles. Leverage expertise and content creation to attract networking opportunities instead of chasing them at events. Choose smaller, more focused networking events and prepare thoroughly for interactions. Use follow-up and relationship maintenance as competitive advantages. Manage energy carefully and build recovery time into networking schedules.

Exercise

Design a networking strategy that works with your introvert tendencies rather than against them. Identify five industry professionals you'd like to know better and reach out for individual coffee meetings rather than trying to connect at group events. Develop a content creation or expertise-sharing strategy that positions you as a resource others want to connect with. Track the quality and business results of these focused networking efforts compared to traditional event-based networking approaches.

Chapter19: International and Remote Networking

Building relationships across time zones and cultures requires completely different strategies than local networking. I learned this the hard way when I tried to apply my standard networking approach to international business relationships and failed miserably.

My first attempt at international networking was a disaster.

I scheduled calls at convenient times for me without considering the other person's time zone.

I used American business communication styles that came across as pushy and inappropriate in other cultures.

I made assumptions about decision-making processes that were completely wrong for the countries I was dealing with.

The wake-up call came when a potential business partner in Japan stopped responding to my emails entirely. Through a mutual contact, I learned that my direct communication style and aggressive follow-up had been perceived as disrespectful. I had destroyed a valuable relationship before it even started.

That experience forced me to completely rethink my approach to international networking. I began researching business cultures, studying communication preferences, and adapting my networking style to different cultural contexts.

The time zone challenge is more complex than just scheduling calls at mutually convenient times. When you're networking across multiple time zones, you need to think about response times, meeting cadences, and the rhythm of business communication.

In the United States, we expect quick responses to emails and frequent check-ins. In many other cultures, business relationships develop more slowly and require patience. What feels like appropriate follow-up in New York might feel like harassment in Tokyo or London.

I learned to adjust my communication frequency based on the cultural norms of the people I was networking with. Europeans often prefer fewer, more substantive communications rather than frequent brief check-ins. Asian business cultures sometimes require longer relationship-building periods before discussing business opportunities.

The technology choices for international networking matter more than most people realize. Email works everywhere, but the platforms people use for instant messaging, video calls, and social networking vary significantly by country and culture.

WhatsApp is essential for business communication in much of Europe and Latin America but barely used in professional contexts in the United States. WeChat dominates business networking in China but is irrelevant in most other markets. LinkedIn is powerful in North America and Europe but less effective in many Asian and African markets.

I had to learn which platforms mattered in each market I was trying to network in. This meant creating accounts on messaging apps I'd never used and learning the etiquette for professional communication on platforms that were completely foreign to me.

Language barriers create networking challenges that go beyond just translation. Even when someone speaks excellent English, they might prefer to receive written communications in their native language for complex business discussions.

I started using professional translation services for important international networking communications. The cost was minimal compared to the potential value of the relationships, and it showed respect for the other person's communication preferences.

Cultural differences in relationship building can make or break international networking efforts. American networking tends to be transactional and goal oriented. We meet people, identify mutual opportunities, and move quickly toward business discussions.

Many other cultures require much longer relationship-building periods. Personal trust must be established before business trust. Family, education, and shared experiences matter more than professional credentials and business opportunities.

I learned to invest more time in personal relationship building when networking internationally. This meant longer conversations about non-business topics, more social interactions, and patience with slower business development timelines.

The concept of networking itself varies dramatically across cultures. In some countries, formal business networks and associations dominate professional relationship building. In others, family connections and educational relationships are more important than professional networking.

Understanding these differences helps you approach international networking appropriately. Trying to apply American-style networking in cultures where business relationships are built differently will mark you as an outsider who doesn't understand local customs.

Remote networking, even within the same country, requires different skills than in-person relationship building. You lose the subtle communication cues that come from body language, facial expressions, and physical presence.

Video calls help bridge this gap, but they're not perfect substitutes for in-person interaction. The delayed audio, technical glitches, and artificial nature of video communication can make relationship building more difficult.

I compensate for these limitations by being more intentional about relationship building in remote networking situations. I schedule longer calls to allow for a more natural conversation flow. I use multiple communication channels to maintain contact. I look for opportunities to meet remotely networked contacts in person when possible.

The follow-up approach for international and remote networking requires more structure than local networking.

When you can't bump into someone at industry events or drop by their office, you need systematic communication to maintain relationships.

I use calendar reminders to ensure regular contact with international networking contacts. The frequency varies based on cultural norms and relationship strength, but I never let important international relationships go over three months without meaningful contact.

Trust building across distances and cultures takes longer and requires different evidence than local networking. People need more proof of your competence and character when they can't observe you in person or get references from mutual acquaintances in their local market.

I invest more time in demonstrating my expertise and reliability to international networking contacts. This might mean providing more detailed proposals, sharing more comprehensive case studies, or making additional introductions to establish credibility.

Time zone coordination becomes a strategic consideration for international networking. I learned to use time zone differences to my advantage rather than seeing them as obstacles.

When I'm networking with people in Asia, I can send emails at the end of my workday that arrive at the beginning of theirs. This creates a natural rhythm of communication that doesn't require either party to work outside normal business hours.

The economic and legal differences between countries affect international networking in ways that domestic networkers never consider. Currency fluctuations, international payment systems, tax implications, and legal frameworks all influence how business relationships develop.

I had to educate myself about these factors when building international networks. Understanding the business environment in different countries helped me have more informed conversations and avoid suggesting arrangements that wouldn't work because of local constraints.

Cultural holidays and business calendars vary dramatically across countries. What looks like a good time to reach out to international contacts might coincide with major holidays or vacation periods in their country.

I keep international calendars for the major markets I network in and plan my outreach accordingly. Respecting cultural calendars shows awareness and consideration that strengthens relationship building.

The compound effect of international networking can be dramatic once you establish credibility in a new market. One strong relationship often leads to introductions throughout an entire business network in that country or region.

But this process takes time and patience. International networking relationships might take years to develop into business opportunities. The people who succeed at international networking think in terms of decades, not quarters.

Remote networking tools continue to evolve and improve the possibilities for building relationships across distances. Virtual reality, improved video conferencing, and AI-powered translation are making international networking more accessible and effective.

But the fundamental principles remain the same. You need to understand cultural differences, respect communication preferences, invest time in relationship building, and show value consistently.

International and remote networking isn't harder than local networking. It's different. The people who succeed adapt their approach to these differences rather than trying to force their standard networking methods to work in inappropriate contexts.

Recap

International and remote networking requires adapting your approach to different time zones, cultures, communication preferences, and business practices. Research cultural norms for business communication and relationship building in each market. Use appropriate technology platforms for each region and consider professional translation for important communications. Allow more time for trust building and relationship development across distances and cultures. Maintain systematic follow-up processes to overcome the lack of casual interaction opportunities.

Exercise

Identify three international markets or remote professionals you'd like to network with. Research the business culture, preferred communication platforms, and relationship-building norms for each market. Adapt your standard networking approach to respect these cultural differences. Schedule initial conversations at times convenient for them rather than you, and track how cultural adaptation affects the quality of relationships you build compared to your standard networking approach.

Chapter 20: Why Cold Outreach Is Not Networking (But How to Make It Work Anyway)

Cold outreach is not networking. Let's get that straight right up front. When you send unsolicited messages to strangers asking for jobs, partnerships, or favors, you're not building relationships. You're interrupting people and hoping they'll help someone they don't know, like, or trust.

But sometimes cold outreach is necessary. When you're starting out, changing careers, or entering new markets, you don't have existing relationships to leverage. You need to create connections from scratch.

The key is understanding the difference between cold outreach and networking, then using cold outreach to start relationships that can eventually become genuine networks.

I've sent thousands of cold emails and messages throughout my career. Most got ignored. Some got hostile responses. A few led to meaningful conversations and long-term relationships. The difference wasn't luck. It was approach.

Cold outreach fails when you treat it like networking.

You can't skip the relationship-building phase and jump straight to asking for help.

You can't pretend to have a connection when none exists.

You can't fake the know, like, and trust factors that make networking effective.

Cold outreach works when you use it to plant seeds for future relationships rather than trying to harvest immediate benefits.

The worst cold outreach I receive follows the same template: brief introduction, mention of something we supposedly have in common, immediate request for a meeting or favor, and a presumptuous assumption that I'll want to help.

These messages fail because they're fundamentally selfish. The sender wants something from me but offers nothing in return. They haven't done any real research about what I do or how they might be helpful. They're just throwing out a net and hoping something gets caught.

The cold outreach that gets my attention is different. It shows genuine research into my work, offers something of value, and asks for something reasonable in return. It doesn't pretend we have a relationship when we don't.

A consultant who specialized in retail technology sent me an email after reading several of my LinkedIn articles about my Trader Joe's experience. His message was straightforward: he'd found my insights valuable, had a specific question about point-of-sale system implementation based on something I'd written, and wondered if I'd be willing to share my perspective on a brief call.

He didn't pretend we knew each other.

He didn't immediately pitch his services.

He didn't ask for introductions or job referrals.

He just wanted to learn from my experience and was respectful in asking.

I took the call because he'd done his homework, asked for something reasonable, and approached the interaction as a peer rather than a supplicant. The conversation led to several more discussions, referrals in both directions, and an ongoing professional relationship.

Effective cold outreach requires three things: research, value, and reasonable requests.

Research means understanding who you're contacting and why your message applies to them. This goes beyond reading their LinkedIn profile. You need to understand their current challenges, recent achievements, and professional interests well enough to craft a message that feels personally relevant.

Value means offering something useful rather than just asking for help. This could be industry insights, relevant connections, useful resources, or simply an interesting perspective on something they care about. The value doesn't need to be huge, but it needs to be genuine.

Reasonable requests means asking for something proportionate to your existing relationship, which in cold outreach is zero. You can ask for a brief conversation, specific advice, or a small favor. You can't ask for job referrals, major time commitments, or access to their network.

Timing matters enormously in cold outreach. The best time to reach out to someone is when they've just achieved something significant, published something interesting, or announced a new role or project. These moments create natural conversation starters and show that your outreach is timely rather than random.

I track industry news and social media activity to identify these timing opportunities. When someone in my field publishes an article, gets promoted, or announces a new initiative, that's often the perfect time to reach out with genuine congratulations and relevant insights.

The follow-up approach in cold outreach is crucial. If someone doesn't respond to your initial message, you have maybe one chance to follow up appropriately. The follow-up should add new value or provide a different angle, not just repeat your original request.

Most people follow up by asking if the person received their first message or by escalating the urgency of their request. This is backwards. The follow-up should make your message more valuable, not more annoying.

Cold outreach should never feel pushy or desperate. The moment you start chasing people, making multiple attempts to connect, or trying to guilt them into responding, you've crossed the line from professional outreach into mild harassment.

The mindset for effective cold outreach is abundance rather than scarcity. You're not dependent on any single person responding. You're planting many seeds, knowing that only a few will grow into meaningful relationships.

This abundance mindset shows in your messaging. You're not begging for attention or trying to convince someone they should help you. You're offering value and suggesting a mutually beneficial interaction.

Platform choice matters in cold outreach. LinkedIn messages often get better response rates than emails because people expect professional communication there. However, LinkedIn's messaging restrictions and the volume of spam make it harder to stand out.

Email can be more effective if you can find the right address and craft a subject line that gets opened. Twitter and other social platforms work for certain industries but require different approaches.

The conversion rate for cold outreach is always low. If you get a 1% or 2% response rate to well-crafted, targeted messages, you're doing well. Most cold outreach gets ignored, and that's normal.

The goal isn't to maximize response rates. What you're aiming for is to start a few high-quality relationships that provide value. One meaningful connection out of 150 cold outreach attempts is a successful campaign.

Cold outreach works best when combined with content creation and thought leadership. When you regularly publish insights, analysis, or helpful resources, cold outreach becomes warmer because people already know who you are.

I had much more success with cold outreach after I started writing regularly about my industry experience. People had context for who I was and why my perspective might be valuable, which made them more likely to engage.

The long-term strategy for cold outreach is to make it unnecessary. Every successful cold outreach interaction should begin a relationship that reduces your need for future cold outreach. You're building a network that will provide warm introductions and referrals.

Cold outreach is a tool for getting started, not a permanent networking strategy. If you're still doing significant amounts of cold outreach after several years in an industry, you're not building relationships effectively.

The professionals who succeed with cold outreach understand its limitations and use it appropriately. They don't confuse it with networking, they don't rely on it exclusively, and they don't use it as an excuse to avoid the hard work of building genuine relationships.

Use cold outreach to start conversations, not to ask for favors.

Use it to show value, not to extract it.

Use it to begin relationships, not to replace them.

When done correctly, cold outreach can open doors that lead to real networking opportunities. But it's never a substitute for authentic relationship building that creates lasting professional success.

Recap

Cold outreach is not networking but can be a tool to start relationships that may eventually become networking opportunities. Effective cold outreach requires genuine research, offers value rather than just asking for help, and makes reasonable requests proportionate to the lack of an existing relationship. Timing outreach around recent achievements or publications improves response rates. Follow up only once and add new value rather than repeating requests. Maintain an abundance mindset and expect low response rates. Use cold outreach to begin conversations and relationships, not to extract immediate favors.

Exercise

Identify five professionals in your industry who could provide valuable perspectives on challenges you're facing. Research their recent work, achievements, or publications thoroughly. Craft cold outreach messages that reference specific aspects of their work, offer genuine value or insights, and request only brief conversations or advice. Send these messages and track response rates, but more importantly, focus on the quality of conversations that result and whether any lead to ongoing professional relationships.

Chapter 21: AI and Networking

AI is changing how we network, and most people are using it incorrectly. They're treating AI like a shortcut to avoid the hard work of building genuine relationships. That's missing the point entirely.

AI can't network for you. It can't build trust, create authentic connections, or replace the human elements that make networking valuable. But it can make you more effective at the tactical parts of relationship building.

When I started experimenting with AI tools for networking, I made the same mistake everyone else was making. I tried to use ChatGPT to write personalized LinkedIn messages and emails. The results were garbage. Generic, obviously AI-generated text that screamed, "I didn't care enough to write this myself."

The problem wasn't the AI. The problem was how I was using it.

AI excels at research, organization, and analysis. It's terrible at authenticity and relationship building. Once I understood this distinction, I used AI to improve my networking effectiveness.

Research is where AI shines brightest for networking. I can feed AI information about someone I want to connect with and get insights that would take hours to compile manually.

Give ChatGPT a LinkedIn profile, recent articles someone has written, and their company's press releases, and it can identify common interests, recent achievements, and potential conversation starters in minutes rather than hours.

But here's the crucial part: I use that research to inform of genuine outreach that I write myself. AI helps me understand who I'm talking to. It doesn't write the actual message.

AI might identify that someone recently spoke at a conference about a topic I'm interested in, published an article about challenges in their industry, or got promoted to a new role. That gives me genuine reasons to reach out and specific topics to discuss.

The message I send references these real details, but it's written in my voice with my authentic interest in the conversation. AI provided the intelligence. I provided the humanity.

Contact management is another area where AI adds real value. Modern CRM systems use AI to track interaction history, remind you to follow up with contacts, and suggest optimal timing for outreach.

I use AI-powered tools to analyze my networking patterns and identify relationships that need attention. The system can flag contacts I haven't spoken to in six months, remind me of commitments I made to follow up on specific topics, and suggest people to reconnect with based on recent news or changes in their companies.

This isn't AI doing the networking. It's AI helping me be more systematic and consistent in maintaining relationships I've already built.

Content creation for networking can benefit from AI help, but only if you use it correctly. AI can help brainstorm topics, research industry trends, and identify what questions your network might be asking.

I might ask AI to analyze recent discussions in my industry and identify themes that keep coming up. This helps me create content that addresses genuine problems people are facing rather than just promoting myself.

But the actual content must be authentically mine. AI can suggest topics and provide research, but the insights, experiences, and perspectives must come from me. People connect with authentic expertise, not AI-generated generic advice.

Event networking is where AI can provide significant tactical advantages. Before attending conferences or virtual events, I use AI to research speakers, analyze attendee lists when available, and identify the most valuable sessions to attend.

AI can process information about dozens of speakers in minutes, highlighting their backgrounds, recent work, and areas of expertise. This helps me prioritize which sessions to attend and the people I most want to connect with.

During virtual events, AI transcription tools can help me capture key points from presentations and identify important quotes or insights to reference in follow-up conversations.

But the actual networking still happens through human interaction. AI helps me be more prepared and focused, not more automated.

Social media monitoring is another area where AI provides networking advantages. AI tools can track mentions of your name, company, or areas of expertise across multiple platforms, alerting you to opportunities for engagement.

When someone mentions a topic you're knowledgeable about, AI can flag it so you can join the conversation with genuine value to add. When potential networking contacts post about challenges you can help with, AI can surface those opportunities.

Use AI to identify relevant conversations, not to participate in them automatically. Automated responses and generic comments are networking poison. AI should alert you to opportunities. You should respond with authentic human engagement.

Email management represents both the biggest opportunity and the biggest danger of AI in networking. AI can help you organize, prioritize, and track networking emails. It can remind you to respond, flag important messages, and maintain context across long email threads.

What AI shouldn't do is write your emails for you. Relationship building requires authenticity, and AI-generated messages feel inauthentic even when they're technically well written.

The professionals who will succeed with AI-enhanced networking are those who understand this balance. They use AI for research, organization, and analysis while keeping the actual relationship building completely human.

Those who try to automate the human elements will fail because networking is basically about trust and authenticity. You can't outsource trust to an algorithm.

AI will continue to develop and provide new capabilities for networking support. But the fundamentals of relationship building won't change. People do business with people they trust and respect. AI can help you be more informed, organized, and strategic in your relationship building, but it can't build relationships for you.

Use AI to do research that makes your conversations more meaningful.

Use it to stay organized so you can maintain more relationships effectively.

Use it to identify opportunities you might otherwise miss.

But when it comes to the actual work of building trust, demonstrating authenticity, and creating genuine connections, that's still entirely human work.

The future of networking isn't human versus AI. It's humans enhanced by AI, using technology to be more effective at the human work of building relationships.

Recap

AI can enhance networking through research, organization, and analysis but cannot replace the human elements of relationship building. Use AI to research contacts, manage follow-ups, identify networking opportunities, and analyze industry trends. Never use AI to write networking messages or automate relationship building. The most effective approach combines AI-powered intelligence with authentic human interaction. AI helps you be more prepared and systematic, but trust and authenticity remain entirely human responsibilities.

Exercise

Choose one AI tool that could help with your networking research or organization. Experiment with using it to research five people in your industry you'd like to connect with, identifying common interests and recent activities. Then write completely human, personalized outreach messages based on that research. Compare the quality of these informed conversations with your typical networking outreach.

Chapter 22: AI Transcription and Networking

AI transcription has become a game changer for networking, but most people don't realize its potential. They think of transcription as a convenience feature for recording meetings. They're missing genuine opportunities.

AI transcription transforms how you capture, organize, and leverage networking conversations. It's like having a perfect memory and a research assistant rolled into one tool.

I started using AI transcription for networking calls after missing a critical detail during an important conversation. I was so focused on maintaining the relationship and asking good questions that I forgot to write down the name of someone they mentioned who could help with a project I was working on.

That mistake taught me that trying to take detailed notes during networking conversations hurts relationship building. When you're writing, you're not fully present. When you're not fully present, you can't build genuine connections.

AI transcription solved this problem completely. Now I can focus entirely on the person I'm talking to while the AI captures every detail of our conversation.

Transcription is just the starting point. The actual power comes from how you use those transcripts for networking follow-up and relationship management.

After each networking conversation, I feed the transcript into ChatGPT with specific prompts. I ask it to identify action items, extract names of people mentioned, note specific challenges the person discussed, list any to do items, and highlight any offers of help or collaboration they made.

This gives me a structured summary that I can reference months later when following up. Instead of generic "How are things going?" emails, I can send specific follow-ups that reference our previous conversation: "How did the product launch you mentioned go?" or "Did you end up connecting with that investor you were considering?"

These specific follow-ups show that I was listening and that I remember details about their business. This level of attention is rare in networking, which makes it powerful for building relationships.

AI transcription also captures networking opportunities that I would have missed otherwise. During a 45-minute conversation, someone might mention five different people who could be valuable connections, three industry events worth attending, and two business challenges where I could provide help.

Without transcription, I might remember the major topics we discussed but miss these specific opportunities. With transcription, I can extract every potential networking lead from a single conversation.

The transcript becomes a networking database. I can search through months of conversations to find people who mentioned specific skills, companies, or interests. When someone in my network asks for a referral, I can quickly find relevant connections from past conversations.

When a client needed a graphic designer who specialized in healthcare branding, I searched my transcripts for "graphic design" and "healthcare" and found three different people who had mentioned working in that exact niche during various networking calls.

Virtual event transcription takes this concept to the next level. Most virtual event tools, such as Zoom, now offer AI transcription of presentations and panel discussions. I download these transcripts and use AI to analyze them for networking insights.

I can identify speakers who discussed topics relevant to my work, extract questions from the audience that revealed potential networking targets, and find specific quotes or statistics to reference in follow-up conversations.

After attending a virtual conference, I might identify ten potential networking contacts from the transcript analysis alone, each with specific conversation starters based on their questions or comments during the event.

Group conversation transcription presents unique networking opportunities. During virtual networking events or group calls, I can transcribe the entire conversation and then analyze which participants showed expertise in areas relevant to my business.

Instead of trying to remember who said what during a chaotic group discussion, I have a complete record that I can analyze for follow-up opportunities. I can reach out to specific participants and reference their insights from the group conversation.

Be transparent about transcription when it's appropriate. For one-on-one networking calls, I always ask permission before recording and explain how I use transcripts to follow up more effectively. Most people appreciate that I'm taking our conversation seriously enough to want to remember the details.

For existing clients, the statement of work states that meetings will be recorded and AI will analyze them. This eliminates the need to ask permission for each meeting.

For virtual events and group calls where recording is standard practice, transcription is just making better use of information that's already being captured.

AI transcription also helps with content creation for networking. I can analyze transcripts from multiple networking conversations to identify common themes and challenges that people in my network are facing.

This insight helps me create content that addresses actual problems rather than guessing what my audience wants to hear. When five different people mention the same challenge during networking calls, that's a clear signal for content topics.

I can also quote insights from networking conversations in my content, with permission, which adds authenticity and shows that I'm actively engaged with my professional community.

The efficiency gains from AI transcription are substantial. What used to take an hour of manual note review after each networking conversation now takes fifteen minutes of AI-assisted analysis. This allows me to have more networking conversations because the follow-up work is streamlined.

Integration with CRM systems amplifies the value of AI transcription. Many modern CRM tools can automatically import transcript summaries, action items, and contact information mentioned during calls.

This creates a comprehensive relationship management system where every networking interaction is documented, searchable, and actionable. Nothing falls through the cracks because the AI captured and organized everything.

The analysis capabilities keep improving. Current AI tools can identify sentiment, extract commitments, flag follow-up dates, and even suggest optimal timing for re-engagement based on conversation patterns.

Some tools can analyze your networking conversations and provide insights about your networking effectiveness. Which types of conversations lead to the most follow-up opportunities? What topics generate the most engagement? How does your networking approach compare to benchmarks?

Privacy and ethics are critical considerations with AI transcription. Always get consent before recording networking conversations. Be transparent about how you use transcripts. Respect confidential information shared during conversations.

Store transcripts securely and delete them when they're no longer needed. Use AI transcription to build better relationships, not to create surveillance or make people uncomfortable.

The networking professionals who master AI transcription will have a significant advantage. They'll remember more details, follow up more effectively, and identify more opportunities from every conversation.

But technology is just a tool. The fundamental work of building trust, providing value, and maintaining authentic relationships still requires human judgment and genuine care for other people's success.

AI transcription makes you a better networker by helping you be more organized, thorough, and responsive. It doesn't make you a networker. That's still human work.

Recap

AI transcription captures detailed records of networking conversations, enabling better follow-up and relationship management. Use transcription combined with AI to extract action items, contact references, and specific details for personalized follow-up.

Virtual event transcripts provide networking opportunities through speaker insights and audience analysis. Always get consent for recording and be transparent about how you use transcripts. Combine transcription with CRM systems for comprehensive relationship tracking. The technology enhances organization and follow-up but doesn't replace genuine relationship building.

Exercise

Record and transcribe your next three networking conversations (with permission). Use AI to analyze each transcript for action items, mentioned contacts, specific challenges discussed, and follow-up opportunities. Compare the quality and specificity of your follow-up emails based on transcript analysis versus your typical post-conversation outreach. Track which generates better responses and continued engagement.

Chapter 23: How Not to Network with AI

AI is making networking worse for most people. They're using it as a crutch to avoid the hard work of building genuine relationships, and it shows. Badly.

I've received dozens of obviously AI-generated LinkedIn messages, emails, and connection requests. They all have the same sterile, overly polite tone that screams, "I didn't care enough to write this myself." These messages get deleted immediately.

If you're using AI to automate your networking outreach, you're not networking. You're spamming.

The worst offenders are people who use AI to mass-generate personalized messages. They feed ChatGPT someone's LinkedIn profile and ask it to write a connection request that mentions specific details about the person's background.

These messages sound personalized on the surface, but they feel hollow. They mention the right details but lack any genuine interest or authentic voice. It's like getting a form letter that has your name inserted in the right places.

I received one of these messages from someone who clearly used AI to analyze my LinkedIn profile. The message referenced my experience at Trader Joe's, mentioned my writing background, and even brought up a specific article I'd published. But it felt completely artificial.

The sender had no actual interest in connecting with me. They just wanted to show that they'd done their homework. When I didn't respond, they followed up with another obviously AI-generated message asking if I'd received their first one.

This approach fails because it's transactional rather than relational. The sender treats networking like a numbers game where the purpose centers on sending as many "personalized" messages as possible. They're not trying to build relationships. They're trying to optimize their outreach efficiency.

AI-generated content for networking suffers from the same problem. People use ChatGPT to write LinkedIn posts, articles, and comments that are technically well written but completely generic.

These posts get engagement because they hit all the right keywords and follow proven formulas for social media success. But they don't build genuine relationships because there's no authentic personality behind them.

I can spot AI-generated LinkedIn content immediately. It has a distinctive tone that's overly enthusiastic, uses buzzwords inappropriately, and makes generic statements that could apply to anyone in any industry.

The comments are even worse. People use AI to generate responses to other people's posts, creating fake engagement that adds nothing to the conversation. These comments are usually variations of "Great insights! This really resonates with me. Thanks for sharing!"

This behavior is networking poison. It turns LinkedIn into a wasteland of fake interactions where nobody is communicating with anyone else. Everyone's just broadcasting AI-generated content into the void.

Automated follow-up sequences are another way people misuse AI for networking. They create chatbots or automated email sequences that "nurture" networking relationships without any human involvement.

I've been added to several of these sequences after connecting with someone on LinkedIn. I receive a series of emails over several weeks, each one supposedly building the relationship and providing value.

These emails are professionally written and contain useful information, but they're completely impersonal. There's no opportunity for genuine conversation or relationship building. It's just marketing automation disguised as networking.

All these approaches treat networking as a marketing problem rather than a relationship problem. The focus is on efficiency, scale, and optimization rather than on understanding and helping other people.

AI amplifies this mistake by making it easier to send more messages, create more content, and automate more interactions. But quantity doesn't create quality in networking. More fake interactions don't lead to better relationships.

Some people use AI to research their networking targets so thoroughly that they come across as stalkers. They know everything about the person's background, recent activities, and interests before they ever have a conversation.

This over-preparation kills spontaneity and makes conversations feel scripted. The other person can sense that you've done extensive research on them, which feels invasive rather than flattering.

Good networking research involves understanding enough about someone to have a meaningful conversation, not memorizing their entire professional history. AI makes it too easy to cross the line from helpful preparation into creepy surveillance.

Social media monitoring taken too far creates the same problem. Some people use AI to track every mention, post, and activity of their networking targets, then use this information to insert themselves into conversations inappropriately.

They show up in comment threads with responses that are too knowledgeable or too perfectly timed.

They reference things the person posted weeks ago in contexts where it makes little sense.

They show that they're watching rather than naturally engaging.

This behavior destroys trust instead of building it. People want to network with individuals who are genuinely interested in them, not with people who are systematically monitoring their online activity.

Another common mistake is using AI to fake expertise or knowledge you don't have. People generate content about topics they don't understand, participate in discussions about subjects they're not qualified to discuss, and offer advice they're not capable of giving.

This approach backfires quickly when the conversation moves beyond surface-level generalities. You can't build professional relationships based on artificial expertise. Eventually, your lack of actual knowledge becomes obvious.

The worst AI networking mistake is trying to scale relationships. People think that if they can use AI to manage more connections, automate more interactions, and engage with more content, they'll build a bigger and better network.

But networking doesn't scale through automation. Relationships require personal attention, genuine care, and authentic interaction. You can't maintain meaningful relationships with hundreds of people through AI-assisted efficiency.

The professionals who succeed with AI networking are those who use it sparingly and strategically. They might use AI for research and organization, but they keep all actual relationship building completely human.

They understand that AI can help them be more prepared and organized, but it can't make them more trustworthy, likeable, or genuinely helpful. Those qualities only come through authentic human interaction.

If you're using AI to write your networking messages, generate your content, automate your follow-up, or fake your expertise, you're not networking. You're performing a caricature of networking that will damage your professional reputation.

People can sense authenticity, and they can sense it when it's missing. AI-powered networking fails because it prioritizes efficiency over genuineness, scale over depth, and automation over relationship building.

Use AI to help you be more organized and better prepared. Don't use it to replace the human work of building trust and creating authentic connections.

Recap

Avoid using AI to write networking messages, generate content, or automate relationship building. AI-generated outreach feels hollow and inauthentic even when technically well-written. Mass personalization using AI research comes across as creepy rather than thoughtful. Automated follow-up sequences and chatbots destroy rather than build relationships. Over-researching networking targets makes conversations feel scripted and invasive. Never use AI to fake expertise you don't possess. Focus on authenticity and genuine human connection rather than efficiency and scale.

Exercise

Review your recent networking outreach and content creation. Identify any messages, posts, or interactions where you used AI help. Analyze whether these AI-assisted communications generated meaningful responses and relationship building compared to your completely human-written outreach. If you've been using AI for networking communication, stop for one month and compare the quality of relationships and responses you build through purely human interaction.

Chapter 24: Modern Tools and Systems

Many business professionals still manage their networking as if it's 1995. They keep business cards in desk drawers, rely on memory for follow-up, and wonder why their networking efforts don't produce consistent results. Meanwhile, their competitors are using modern tools and systems to build relationships more effectively and efficiently.

The technology available for networking today would have seemed like science fiction when I started my career. CRM systems that track every interaction, automation tools that remind you to follow up, AI that helps research contacts and craft personalized messages. These tools don't replace human relationship building, but they make it much more systematic and scalable.

I resisted networking technology for years because I thought relationship building should be purely personal. I had misjudged the situation. The professionals who succeed at networking today use technology to be more organized, more consistent, and more helpful to their networks.

Understanding what technology can and can't do for networking is crucial. Technology excels at organization, reminders, research, and routine communication. It fails miserably at authenticity, trust building, and genuine relationship development.

Customer Relationship Management systems designed for networking go far beyond contact management. Modern CRM platforms track interaction history, remind you to follow up with contacts, and help you identify networking opportunities based on relationship patterns and business intelligence.

I started using CRM for networking after watching a consultant manage relationships with over 500 industry contacts systematically. He knew when he'd last spoken with each person, what they'd discussed, and what follow-up actions were needed. His networking was more effective because he was more organized.

The CRM captured every email exchange, phone call, and meeting. When someone called him six months after their last conversation, he could quickly review their history and pick up the relationship exactly where it had left off.

This systematic approach eliminated the awkward situations where you can't remember details about previous conversations or forget to follow up on commitments you made to networking contacts.

Automation tools for networking handle routine tasks that would otherwise fall through the cracks. Birthday reminders, follow-up scheduling, social media monitoring, and content sharing can all be automated to ensure consistent relationship maintenance.

I use automation to remind me when I haven't contacted important networking relationships in predetermined time periods. High-priority contacts get quarterly reminders, medium-priority contacts get semi-annual reminders, and low-priority contacts get annual check-ins.

The automation doesn't write messages for me. It just ensures I don't let relationships deteriorate from neglect. When the reminder pops up, I craft a personalized message based on our relationship history and their current situation.

Social media automation tools monitor mentions of your name, company, or areas of expertise across platforms. This allows you to join relevant conversations and show your expertise to broader audiences than your immediate network.

I have alerts set for industry keywords and the names of key networking contacts. When someone in my network posts about a topic I can contribute to, I receive a notification and can engage with their content meaningfully.

Research tools powered by AI can provide background information about networking contacts that would take hours to compile manually. These tools aggregate public information about people's backgrounds, recent activities, and business interests from multiple sources.

Before important networking meetings or conversations, I use these tools to understand someone's current challenges, recent achievements, and professional interests. This research helps me ask better questions and identify potential ways to help them.

Research tools don't replace getting to know people personally. They provide context that makes personal conversations more productive and helps me offer more relevant assistance.

Email marketing platforms designed for relationship building rather than mass marketing help maintain contact with your network systematically. These platforms allow you to segment your contacts, personalize messages, and track engagement without sending impersonal blast emails.

I use these platforms to share valuable content with my network, announce relevant business updates, and maintain visibility between individual conversations. The key is providing value rather than promoting yourself.

The platforms track who opens messages, clicks links, and responds to your communications. This data helps you understand which content resonates with your network and which contacts are most engaged with your relationship-building efforts.

Calendar integration tools streamline the process of scheduling networking meetings and following up on commitments. These tools eliminate the email back-and-forth typically required to coordinate calendars and reduce friction in relationship building.

I share calendar links with networking contacts that allow them to book meetings directly. This makes me more accessible and increases the likelihood that relationship-building conversations happen.

The tools also track commitments made during meetings and send reminders to ensure follow-through on promises.

Reliability in small matters builds trust for larger business relationships.

AI-powered tools can assist with networking research, content creation, and message personalization, but they can't replace human judgment and authenticity. Use AI to become more informed and organized, not to automate relationship building.

I use AI to research industry trends that might interest my networking contacts, analyze the best times to reach out to people based on their response patterns, and identify potential connections between people in my network who might benefit from knowing each other.

But the actual conversations, relationship building, and value creation remain entirely human activities. AI provides intelligence that makes these activities more effective, but it can't perform them for you.

Content management systems help you share valuable insights with your network consistently without overwhelming people with too much information. These systems allow you to create content calendars, schedule social media posts, and track which content generates the most networking engagement.

I create content that addresses common challenges faced by people in my network, then use these systems to share it across appropriate platforms at optimal times. The goal is to be helpful to my network rather than to promote myself.

The systems track which content generates comments, shares, and direct messages from networking contacts. This engagement often leads to deeper conversations and relationship development opportunities.

Digital business card platforms eliminate the need for physical cards while providing much more information and functionality. These platforms allow contacts to save your information directly to their phones and access updated contact details, social media profiles, and relevant content.

I use digital cards that include links to my recent articles, case studies, and calendar booking system. This makes it easier for networking contacts to stay connected and engage with my work between meetings.

The platforms track when people view your digital card, which information they access, and how they prefer to stay in touch. This data helps you tailor your follow-up approach to each contact's preferences.

Integration between networking tools creates seamless workflows that reduce administrative overhead and improve relationship management effectiveness. When your CRM, email platform, calendar system, and social media tools work together, you can manage larger networks more efficiently.

I have integrated systems that automatically capture contact information from meetings, track email interactions in my CRM, and schedule follow-up reminders based on relationship priorities. This integration ensures no networking opportunities fall through the administrative cracks.

The key is choosing tools that work well together rather than trying to use the best individual tool for each function. Compatibility and workflow efficiency matter more than having the most sophisticated features.

Analytics and reporting tools help you understand which networking activities produce the best results and deserve more of your time and energy. These tools track relationship development, business outcomes, and networking ROI across different activities and platforms.

I track which types of networking events produce the most valuable contacts, which relationship-building approaches generate the most business referrals, and which content topics create the most networking engagement.

This data helps me focus my limited time on the networking activities that produce the best results while eliminating approaches that don't create meaningful relationships or business opportunities.

Tool selection for networking should focus on systems that enhance rather than replace human relationship building.

Choose tools that make you more organized, informed, and systematic in your networking efforts while maintaining authenticity in your interactions.

The professionals who succeed with networking technology understand that tools are multipliers, not substitutes, for genuine relationship building. They use technology to be more effective at the human work of building trust, providing value, and creating mutual business benefits.

Start with simple tools that address your biggest networking challenges, then expand your toolkit as you become more systematic about relationship building. The goal is to build better relationships more efficiently, not impressing people with your technology stack.

Recap

Modern networking tools enhance relationship building through better organization, automation, and research capabilities. CRM systems track interactions and remind you to follow up consistently. Automation handles routine tasks while preserving authenticity in personal communications. AI assists with research and analysis but can't replace human relationship building. Integration between tools creates efficient workflows for managing larger networks. Analytics help identify which networking activities produce the best results. Choose tools that multiply your relationship-building effectiveness rather than replacing human interaction.

Exercise

Evaluate your current networking organization and identify the biggest inefficiencies in your relationship management process. Choose one modern tool that addresses this challenge, whether it's a CRM system, automation platform, or research tool. Implement the tool for managing your networking activities over the next month and track how it affects your consistency, organization, and relationship-building results. Focus on using technology to enhance rather than replace your human networking efforts.

Chapter 25: Keeping Track of Your Networking Efforts

I was terrible at following up with people I met at conferences and events. I'd come home with a stack of business cards, dump them on my desk, and tell myself I'd reach out to everyone soon. Weeks later, I'd find the cards scattered under papers and couldn't remember half the conversations.

This approach was killing my networking effectiveness. I was meeting people but failing to convert those meetings into ongoing relationships. The problem wasn't that I was bad at networking. The core difficulty lay in the fact that I had no system for managing the relationships I was building.

Everything changed when I started treating networking like any other important business activity. I began tracking my efforts, measuring results, and systematically following up with contacts. My networking became ten times more effective because I stopped letting opportunities slip through the cracks.

Most people wing it when it comes to tracking their networking efforts. They rely on memory, keep contacts in their phone, and hope they'll remember to follow up with important connections. This casual approach guarantees that most networking opportunities get wasted.

Professional networking requires professional systems. You need to capture information about the people you meet, track your interactions with them, and maintain regular contact. This doesn't require expensive software or complicated processes. It just requires consistency.

The basic information you need to capture about each networking contact includes their name, company, role, contact information, where and when you met them, and key details about your conversation. But the most important piece is noting how you can help them and what kind of help they might provide to you.

The importance of this hit me during my computer industry days when I started keeping detailed notes on the back of business cards immediately after conversations. I'd write what we discussed, what challenges they were facing, and any specific ways I might assist them. This made my follow-up emails more personal and relevant.

When I got back to my office, I'd transfer this information into a simple spreadsheet with columns for name, company, contact date, conversation notes, follow-up actions, and next contact date. Nothing fancy, but it kept me organized and ensured I didn't lose track of valuable connections.

The key is to capture this information while it's fresh in your memory. Waiting until the end of the day or the next week means you'll forget important details that could make the difference between a generic follow-up and a meaningful conversation.

"I gotta be consistent, and persistent, and do what I tell people to do, you know, be consistent." - Haleh Houshim

---

During virtual networking events, I keep a document open on my computer and take notes in real time. When someone mentions a specific challenge they're facing or shares an insight, I capture it immediately. This allows me to reference these details in my follow-up communications.

The follow-up tracking is where most people fail completely. They meet someone, exchange contact information, and never reach out again. Or they send one email and give up if they don't get a response. Building relationships requires consistent effort.

I use a simple system to ensure regular follow-up with my networking contacts. Each person gets categorized based on their potential value to my business and my ability to help them. High-priority contacts get quarterly follow-up. Medium-priority contacts get contacted twice a year. Low-priority contacts get an annual check-in.

This might sound calculating, but it's realistic. You can't maintain close relationships with hundreds of people. You need to focus your limited time and energy on the relationships that are most likely to produce mutual value.

The follow-up doesn't need to be complicated. A brief email asking how their business is going, sharing something important, or making an introduction to someone who might help them. The goal is remaining visible and showing that you're thinking about them and their success.

I keep a calendar reminder system that prompts me to reach out to specific contacts on a rotating schedule. This ensures that I'm consistently maintaining relationships rather than only contacting people when I need something from them.

"I like to think of networking more like farming, rather than hunting. If you need a sale to feed your family by Friday, go hunting and make a sale. But if you want to cultivate a garden of ongoing, continuous referrals, you need to network." – Mark O'Donnell

---

Measuring the results of your networking efforts is crucial but often overlooked. Most people attend events, meet people, and do not know whether their networking is producing business results. They treat networking as a social activity rather than a business investment.

I track specific metrics to understand which networking activities are worth my time and which are a waste of effort.

How many new contacts did I make at each event?

How many led to follow-up conversations?

How many resulted in business opportunities or referrals?

This data helped me realize that certain types of events were much more productive than others. Industry conferences with focused audiences generated higher-quality contacts than broad networking mixers. Virtual events often produced better follow-up rates than in-person gatherings because people were more responsive to digital communications.

The tracking also revealed that my networking ROI improved dramatically when I focused on helping others rather than promoting myself. Contacts who received value from our initial interaction were much more likely to respond to follow-up communications and refer opportunities to me.

Modern CRM systems can automate much of this tracking, but you don't need expensive software to get started. A simple spreadsheet or even a notebook can be effective if you use it consistently.

The critical factor is having a system and sticking to it. Whether you use high-tech or low-tech tools matters less than whether you capture information, follow up regularly, and measure results.

Your networking system should also include tracking the help you provide to others. When you make introductions, share resources, or give advice to people in your network, note these actions. This helps you understand your value to others and gives you examples to reference in future conversations.

I maintain a simple log of favors and help I provide to networking contacts. This isn't about keeping score or expecting returns. It's about understanding how I'm contributing to my network and ensuring that I'm consistently adding value to other people's businesses.

The system also helps me identify people who consistently take value from the relationship without providing anything in return. These one-way relationships deserve less time and attention than mutual partnerships where both parties benefit.

Regular review of your networking database is essential. Every quarter, I go through my contact list and update information, remove people who are no longer relevant, and identify relationships that need more attention.

This review process often reveals networking opportunities I've missed. Someone I met six months ago might have changed jobs and moved into a role where they could be more helpful. A contact who wasn't initially valuable might have developed expertise that's now relevant to my business.

The goal isn't to build the largest possible network. It's to build the most valuable network and maintain it effectively. A dozen well-managed relationships will produce better results than a thousand neglected contacts.

Start simple with whatever system you'll use consistently. A notebook that you write in daily is better than sophisticated software that you never update. The key is capturing information about the people you meet and following up systematically to turn those meetings into ongoing relationships.

Recap

Effective networking requires systematic tracking of contacts, conversations, and follow-up actions. Capture key information about each person you meet, including how you can help them and how they might assist you. Implement a regular follow-up schedule based on the potential value of each relationship. Measure the results of your networking efforts to identify which activities produce the best returns. Use whatever system you'll maintain consistently, whether high-tech or low-tech.

Exercise

Set up a simple tracking system for your networking contacts, either using a spreadsheet or CRM software. For the next month, capture detailed information about every new professional contact you make, including conversation notes and potential ways to help each other. Schedule follow-up reminders for each contact and track which networking activities produce the most valuable connections. Review your results at the end of the month to identify patterns and improve your approach.

Chapter 26: Referral Systems

I learned about referrals the hard way when I referred a client to a consultant who completely screwed up the project. The client lost money, the consultant disappeared, and I looked like an idiot for making the introduction. That experience taught me that referrals can either build or destroy your professional reputation.

Most people think giving referrals is simple. Someone asks for a recommendation, you mention a name, and you're done. Wrong. Effective referral systems require careful vetting, clear communication, and ongoing follow-up to protect your reputation and maximize value for everyone involved.

When someone asks me for a referral now, I don't just throw out the first name that comes to mind. I consider whether the person I'm referring can solve the problem, whether they'll treat my contact professionally, and whether the timing is right for both parties.

This became clear from watching my former boss, Steve, operate. When clients asked him for referrals, he'd talk to them about their specific needs, research potential solutions, and often make multiple introductions to give them options. He treated referrals as seriously as any other business recommendation.

Steve's referrals were highly valued because people knew he'd done his homework. When Steve referred someone to you, it meant you were dealing with a vetted professional who understood your situation. This made Steve's network incredibly valuable to everyone in it.

The first rule of giving referrals is to understand the actual need. When someone asks for a recommendation, don't immediately start suggesting names. Ask detailed questions about their situation, budget, timeline, and specific requirements.

A request for "a good accountant" could mean anything from basic bookkeeping for a small business to complex tax planning for a Fortune 500 company. The person who's perfect for one situation might be completely wrong for another.

I once had someone ask me for a web designer referral. Instead of immediately suggesting names, I asked about their budget, timeline, technical requirements, and design preferences. It turned out they needed an e-commerce specialist with experience in their specific industry, not just any web designer.

This conversation helped me refer them to exactly the right person and avoid wasting everyone's time with inappropriate introductions.

The second rule is only to refer people you trust completely. Your reputation is attached to every referral you make. If the person you refer does poor work, misses deadlines, or treats your contact unprofessionally, it reflects badly on you.

I maintain a short list of professionals I refer regularly because I've seen their work and trust their character. I don't refer people based on their marketing materials or what others have told me about them. I refer only people whose work I've experienced personally or who received excellent reviews when I've referred them.

This means I sometimes tell people I don't have a good referral for their specific needs rather than making an introduction I'm not confident about. Saying, "I don't know anyone who specializes in that" protects my reputation and their interests better than referring someone I'm unsure about.

The referral introduction itself requires careful handling. I don't just send an email saying, "You two should meet." I provide context about why I'm making the introduction, what each person brings to the potential relationship, and what I think they might accomplish together.

A good referral introduction explains the specific need, why I think the referred person can help, and gives both parties enough information to have a productive first conversation. I also set expectations about the timeline, budget, and other relevant factors.

I usually send separate emails to each party before making the introduction. This allows me to provide more detailed context and ensures both people are interested in connecting before I bring them together.

Following up on referrals is crucial but often neglected. After making an introduction, I check in with both parties to see how things went. This helps me understand whether my referrals are producing good results and allows me to improve my referral process.

If a referral doesn't work out, I want to know why.

Was it a mismatch in expectations?

Did the referred person not follow through professionally?

Did the timing not work?

This information helps me make better referrals in the future.

When referrals do work out, I make sure both parties know I'm pleased with the result. This reinforces the value of my network and encourages people to come to me for future referrals.

Receiving referrals requires its own set of skills. When someone refers business to you, they're putting their reputation on the line. You need to treat referred prospects better than cold leads because the person making the referral has vouched for you.

I respond to referrals within 24 hours, even if it's just to acknowledge receipt and schedule a proper conversation. I also keep the referring party informed about how things progress, especially if the referral doesn't result in business.

When someone refers a prospect to me who isn't a good fit, I handle the situation carefully. I have a brief conversation with the prospect to understand their needs, explain why I might not be the right solution, and often refer them to someone who can help them.

This approach protects the reputation of the person who made the original referral while demonstrating that I care more about solving problems than making sales.

Building a referral system requires reciprocity. People who regularly refer business to you should receive referrals from you when appropriate opportunities arise. This doesn't mean keeping score, but it does mean being attentive to opportunities to help people who help you.

I keep track of who refers business to me and actively look for ways to return the favor. When I hear about opportunities that might benefit someone in my network, I reach out to see if they're interested in an introduction.

Some of the strongest business relationships I have are built on mutual referrals. We trust each other's judgment, understand each other's ideal clients, and consistently look for ways to help each other grow our businesses.

Referral tracking helps you understand which networking relationships are producing the best business results. I track who refers business to me, what types of referrals they make, and how often those referrals convert to actual business.

This data helps me prioritize my networking efforts and identify the relationships that deserve more of my time and attention. It also helps me understand what types of referrals I'm best positioned to give and receive.

The timing of referrals matters enormously. Referring someone when they're overloaded with work doesn't help anyone. Neither does referring prospects who need immediate help to service providers who are booked months out.

I stay in touch with my referral network about their current capacity and availability. This allows me to make timely referrals that benefit both parties rather than creating frustration.

Industry-specific referral opportunities require special attention. In some fields, referrals between competitors are common and accepted. In others, they're seen as conflicts of interest. Understanding the norms in your industry helps you navigate referral situations appropriately.

I've seen professionals damage their reputations by making referrals that violated industry standards or created ethical conflicts. When in doubt, I ask the person making the request how they want me to handle the situation rather than making assumptions.

Digital referral systems and platforms can automate some aspects of referral management, but they can't replace the human judgment required for quality referrals. Technology can help track referrals and manage introductions, but it can't evaluate whether a referral makes sense.

The most effective referral systems combine technology for organization with human insight for decision making. Use tools to stay organized, but rely on your judgment and relationships to make quality referrals.

Referral fees and commissions create complications that need to be handled transparently. If you receive compensation for referrals, both parties should know about the arrangement upfront. Hidden referral fees destroy trust and damage relationships.

I avoid referral fee arrangements in most situations because they can compromise my objectivity. When I do participate in referral programs, I disclose the arrangement to everyone involved so they can make informed decisions.

The goal of a referral system isn't to maximize the number of introductions you make. It's to make high-quality connections that create value for everyone involved while building your reputation as someone who understands business and cares about helping others succeed.

A few excellent referrals that produce results are worth more than dozens of mediocre introductions that waste everyone's time. Focus on quality over quantity, and your referral network will become one of your most valuable business assets.

Recap

Effective referral systems protect your reputation while creating value for all parties involved. Understand specific needs before making referrals and only refer people you trust completely. Provide context in referral introductions and follow up on results. Treat received referrals as high-priority opportunities and maintain reciprocal relationships with your referral network. Track referral performance to identify the most valuable networking relationships and understand industry-specific referral norms.

Exercise

Create a list of professionals you trust enough to refer to others and identify their specific areas of expertise. For the next month, when anyone asks you for referrals, follow the complete process: understand their specific needs, match them with the right contacts, make proper introductions with context, and follow up on results. Track which referrals produce positive outcomes and which relationships provide the most valuable mutual referrals.

Chapter 27: Maintaining Your Network

Network development is challenging, but relationship maintenance proves more difficult. Most people focus all their energy on meeting new contacts while their existing relationships deteriorate from neglect. They attend networking events constantly but never follow up with the valuable contacts they already have.

This strategy proves counterproductive and wasteful. The relationships you've already built are your most valuable networking assets. They know your work, trust your character, and understand how to help you. Yet most people ignore them while chasing new connections at every industry event.

I learned about network maintenance the hard way when I realized I'd lost touch with dozens of valuable contacts over the years. People who had been helpful colleagues, trusted advisors, and potential business partners had disappeared from my professional life because I hadn't invested in maintaining those relationships.

When I tried to reconnect with some of these contacts years later, many of the relationships had cooled to where they were essentially starting over. The trust and familiarity we'd built through working together had faded because I hadn't maintained regular contact.

Network maintenance isn't about staying in touch with everyone you've ever met. It's about systematically nurturing the relationships that matter most to your business and career goals. This requires prioritization, consistency, and a genuine interest in other people's success.

The first step in network maintenance is categorizing your contacts based on their potential value to your business and your ability to help them. This might sound calculating, but it's realistic. You can't maintain close relationships with hundreds of people.

I divide my network into three categories: core relationships that deserve monthly contact, important relationships that need quarterly touch points, and broader relationships that get annual check-ins. This system ensures I maintain regular contact with my most valuable networking relationships while staying visible to my broader professional network.

Core relationships include people who refer business to me regularly, strategic partners who collaborate with me on projects, industry influencers who affect my business, and trusted advisors who provide valuable guidance. These relationships deserve the most time and attention.

Important relationships include former colleagues who've moved to influential positions, professionals in adjacent industries who occasionally refer opportunities, and potential clients or partners who might become core relationships. These contacts need regular but less frequent engagement.

Broader relationships include people I've met at conferences, former clients who might need services again, and industry contacts who provide market intelligence or occasional referrals. Annual contact keeps me visible without overwhelming my schedule.

Consistent communication schedules are crucial for network maintenance. Without systematic reminders, important relationships will fall through the cracks during busy periods. I use calendar reminders to ensure regular contact with networking relationships based on their priority level.

The reminders don't dictate what I communicate. They ensure I don't let relationships deteriorate from neglect. When a reminder pops up, I review my relationship history with that contact and determine the most appropriate way to reconnect.

Value-added communication keeps network maintenance from feeling like an obligation or pestering. Every interaction with your network should provide some kind of value: useful information, relevant introductions, helpful insights, or simply genuine interest in their success.

I avoid generic "checking in" messages that provide no value to the recipient. Instead, I share articles relevant to their business challenges, introduce them to people who might help them, or ask thoughtful questions about projects they're working on.

This approach makes people look forward to hearing from me rather than viewing my outreach as another networking pitch. When your communications consistently provide value, people are more responsive and engaged.

Social media engagement provides an efficient way to maintain visibility with your network between individual communications. Commenting thoughtfully on LinkedIn posts, sharing relevant content, and engaging with your contacts' business updates keeps you visible without requiring individual outreach.

I spend fifteen minutes each morning engaging with posts from my networking contacts. This consistent engagement keeps me visible to hundreds of people while providing genuine support for their professional activities.

The key is meaningful engagement rather than generic likes or comments. Add insights, ask thoughtful questions, or share relevant experiences that contribute to their conversations.

Content sharing allows you to provide value to your entire network simultaneously while maintaining regular contact. Industry insights, useful resources, and relevant opportunities shared with your network keep you visible while helping multiple people at once.

I send monthly newsletters to my network, sharing industry trends, useful tools, and networking opportunities that might benefit different segments of my contacts. This systematic communication maintains relationships without requiring individual outreach to everyone.

The content should focus on helping your network rather than promoting yourself. People value networking contacts who consistently share useful information more than those who constantly self-promote.

Event-based reconnection opportunities provide natural reasons to renew contact with networking relationships. Industry conferences, company milestones, job changes, and business achievements all create contexts for reaching out to contacts you haven't spoken with recently.

I monitor news and social media updates from my networking contacts to identify these opportunities. When someone gets promoted, speaks at a conference, or announces a business milestone, I reach out with genuine congratulations and use the opportunity to reconnect.

These event-based touches feel natural rather than forced because they're tied to specific developments in their professional lives.

Personal milestone recognition strengthens networking relationships by demonstrating that you see contacts as people rather than just business resources. Work anniversaries, professional achievements, and significant life events all provide opportunities for meaningful contact.

I keep notes about personal information that networking contacts share and acknowledge these milestones appropriately. This might congratulate someone on their child's graduation, ask about a family move they mentioned, or recognize their company's anniversary.

This personal touch differentiates your networking approach from purely transactional relationship management and builds stronger emotional connections.

Referral and introduction opportunities provide the highest-value form of network maintenance. When you connect people in your network who can help each other, you strengthen your relationships with both parties while positioning yourself as a valuable connector.

I actively look for ways to connect people in my network based on their expressed needs and complementary capabilities. These introductions often lead to business relationships that create lasting value for everyone involved.

Being known as someone who makes valuable introductions makes people want to maintain relationships with you and refer opportunities to you in return.

Relationship audit processes help identify which networking relationships need attention and which might no longer deserve your time investment. Quarterly reviews of your networking activities help ensure you're focusing on the most valuable relationships.

I review my contact database every quarter to identify people I haven't spoken with recently, relationships that have become less relevant to my business goals, and new contacts who should be elevated to higher priority categories.

This audit process helps me adjust my networking priorities based on changing business needs and ensures I'm not wasting time on relationships that no longer provide mutual value.

Geographic considerations affect network maintenance strategies, especially for professionals who move frequently or work with distributed networks. Maintaining relationships across time zones and distances requires different approaches than local networking.

I use virtual coffee meetings, scheduled phone calls, and strategic travel planning to maintain relationships with valuable contacts in different locations. The effort required for long-distance relationship maintenance means being even more selective about which relationships deserve this investment.

Digital tools help manage network maintenance systematically, but they can't replace genuine human connection. CRM systems, social media management tools, and communication platforms support relationship maintenance but don't substitute for authentic interest in other people's success.

I use tools to stay organized and ensure consistent contact, but the actual relationship building happens through personalized communication that shows genuine care about each contact's success.

Long-term relationship development requires patience and consistency over years or even decades. The most valuable networking relationships are those that survive job changes, industry shifts, and geographic moves because they're based on mutual respect and genuine professional friendship.

Some of my strongest business relationships have developed over fifteen or twenty years through consistent but not overwhelming contact. These relationships provide support, guidance, and opportunities throughout career transitions and business challenges.

Network maintenance isn't about staying in touch with everyone you've ever met. It's about systematically nurturing the relationships that matter most while remaining visible to your broader professional network. This requires prioritization, consistency, and a genuine commitment to helping others succeed.

The professionals who build lasting career success understand that network maintenance is an ongoing investment that pays dividends for decades. They treat relationship maintenance as seriously as any other crucial business activity.

Recap

Network maintenance requires systematic nurturing of existing relationships rather than constantly chasing new contacts. Categorize contacts by priority and maintain communication schedules for each level. Provide value through every interaction rather than sending generic check-in messages. Use social media engagement and content sharing to maintain visibility efficiently. Leverage event-based opportunities and personal milestones for natural reconnection. Focus on making valuable introductions between contacts. Conduct regular relationship audits to ensure you're investing in the most valuable connections.

Exercise

Audit your current networking relationships and categorize them into core, important, and broader contact groups. Create a maintenance schedule with contact frequencies for each category. For the next three months, follow this schedule while focusing on providing value through each interaction rather than generic outreach. Track which relationships become more responsive and engaged through systematic maintenance versus sporadic contact.

Chapter 28: Measuring Success

Most people do not know whether their networking efforts are working. They attend events, meet people, exchange business cards, and hope something good happens. They treat networking like a social activity instead of a business investment that should produce measurable results.

This casual approach to measuring networking success guarantees mediocre results.

You can't improve what you don't measure.

You can't identify your most valuable networking activities if you don't track outcomes.

You can't justify the time investment in networking if you don't understand the ROI.

I spent years networking without measuring results and wondering why I wasn't getting the business growth I expected. I was busy with networking activities but had no idea which ones were producing value. I was working hard but not smart.

My results improved dramatically after I started treating networking like any other business activity that requires measurement and optimization. I began tracking which events produced valuable contacts, which relationships generated business referrals, and which networking approaches created the best ROI.

The data revealed patterns I never would have noticed otherwise. Some networking events I thought were valuable were a complete waste of time. Other activities I'd dismissed as unimportant were generating significant business results.

This measurement approach transformed my networking effectiveness because it allowed me to focus on activities that produced results while eliminating approaches that didn't create value.

Relationship quality metrics matter more than quantity measurements for networking success. Most people count contacts, connections, and business cards collected, but these vanity metrics don't correlate with business results.

The relationships that generate business value are those where people know you well enough to refer opportunities, trust you enough to make introductions, and understand your capabilities well enough to think of you when relevant needs arise.

I track relationship depth rather than relationship quantity.

How many people in my network would feel comfortable referring a client to me?

How many understand my business well enough to identify excellent opportunities?

How many trust me enough to make introductions to their valuable contacts?

These deeper relationship metrics predict networking success much better than the size of your contact database.

Business outcome tracking connects networking activities to actual revenue and opportunities. Unless you're tracking which networking relationships produce business results, you're just guessing about the value of your relationship-building efforts.

I maintain a simple system that tracks the source of every business inquiry, referral, and opportunity. When someone contacts me about potential work, I document how they found me and which networking relationships contributed to the connection.

This tracking revealed that most of my best business opportunities came from a small percentage of my networking contacts. The 80/20 rule applies strongly to networking: a few relationships generate most of the business value.

Event ROI analysis helps you understand which networking events deserve your time and money. Most professionals attend events based on convenience or habit rather than analyzing which ones produce the best relationship-building results.

I track the number of valuable contacts made at each event, the quality of follow-up conversations, and whether any business opportunities resulted from those connections. This data helps me decide which events to attend regularly and which to skip.

The analysis often reveals surprising results. Expensive high-profile conferences sometimes produce fewer valuable relationships than smaller industry gatherings. Virtual events might generate better follow-up rates than in-person meetings.

Time investment tracking ensures you're allocating networking effort efficiently. Networking can easily consume unlimited amounts of time if you don't establish boundaries and measure productivity.

I track time spent on different networking activities: attending events, follow-up conversations, relationship maintenance, content creation, and social media engagement. This data helps me understand which activities produce the best results per hour invested.

Some networking activities have high upfront time costs but create lasting value. Others require minimal time investment but produce limited results. Understanding these patterns helps you optimize your networking schedule.

Referral source analysis identifies which relationships are most valuable for business development. Some networking contacts refer opportunities regularly, others refer occasionally, and many never refer anything despite years of relationship building.

I track who refers business to me, what types of opportunities they refer, and how often those referrals convert to actual business. This analysis helps me prioritize relationship maintenance efforts and understand which contacts deserve the most attention.

The data also reveals patterns about what types of networking contacts make the best referral sources. Former clients, complementary service providers, and industry colleagues each have different referral patterns and potential.

Content engagement metrics show which networking approaches generate the most relationship-building opportunities. If you create content as part of your networking strategy, you need to measure which topics and formats create the most valuable interactions.

I track which articles, posts, and presentations generate the most comments, direct messages, and follow-up conversations from networking contacts. This data helps me create content that supports relationship building rather than just showing expertise.

Content that starts conversations with potential networking contacts is more valuable than content that generates likes or views but no meaningful engagement.

Pipeline impact measurement connects networking activities to your sales and business development process. Networking should feed your business development pipeline with qualified opportunities, not just creating good social interactions.

I track how networking-sourced opportunities compare to other lead sources in terms of conversion rates, average deal size, and sales cycle length. Networking-generated opportunities often convert at higher rates because they come with built-in trust and credibility.

This analysis helps justify the time investment in networking by demonstrating concrete business impact rather than just relationship-building activity.

Long-term relationship value assessment recognizes that networking benefits often compound. A relationship that doesn't produce immediate business might generate significant value years later through referrals, partnerships, or opportunities.

I maintain longitudinal tracking of networking relationships to understand how they develop. Some contacts become more valuable as their careers advance or their businesses grow. Others become less relevant as industries change or interests diverge.

This long-term perspective helps you invest in relationships that have growth potential while recognizing when to reduce investment in relationships that aren't developing mutual value.

Cost analysis includes both the direct costs of networking events and the opportunity cost of time invested in relationship building. Networking isn't free, even when you're not paying event fees or membership dues.

I calculate the total cost of networking activities including event fees, travel expenses, meal costs, and the value of time invested. This analysis helps me understand the true cost per valuable relationship developed through different networking approaches.

Some networking activities have low direct costs but high time investments. Others have high direct costs but produce results more efficiently. Understanding these trade-offs helps optimize your networking budget.

Competitive advantage measurement assesses whether your networking efforts are creating business advantages over competitors. Networking should provide access to opportunities, information, and relationships that your competitors don't have.

I track whether my networking relationships provide early access to business opportunities, valuable market intelligence, or introductions to key decision makers. These competitive advantages are often the most valuable outcomes of networking investments.

When networking provides unique access to opportunities or information, it creates sustainable business advantages that justify significant time investment.

Goal alignment assessment ensures your networking activities support your business and career objectives. Networking for its own sake is a waste of time if it doesn't advance your professional goals.

I regularly review whether my networking efforts connect me with the right people for my business objectives. Are the relationships I'm building relevant to my target market? Do my networking contacts understand my capabilities and goals?

This assessment sometimes reveals that networking activities aren't aligned with business strategy and need to be adjusted to produce more relevant results.

The measurement approach to networking doesn't make relationship building cold or calculating. It ensures that your networking efforts produce real value for your business while helping you invest time in the most promising relationships.

When you measure networking success systematically, you discover which activities deserve more investment and which approaches waste time and energy. This data-driven approach to relationship building produces better results while requiring less total effort.

Start measuring your networking success with simple metrics that track relationship development and business outcomes. The insights you gain will transform your approach to professional relationship building and dramatically improve your results.

Recap

Measuring networking success requires tracking relationship quality over quantity, business outcomes from networking activities, and ROI from different networking approaches. Monitor which events and activities produce valuable contacts and follow-up opportunities. Track referral sources and conversion rates to identify the most valuable networking relationships. Measure content engagement and pipeline impact to understand which networking strategies generate business results. Include time investment and opportunity costs in networking ROI calculations. Assess whether networking efforts align with business goals and create competitive advantages.

Exercise

Design a simple measurement system for your networking activities that tracks at least three key metrics: relationship development, business outcomes, and time investment. For the next quarter, consistently measure these aspects of your networking efforts. At the end of the period, analyze which networking activities produce the best results and adjust your networking strategy based on the data you've collected. Focus on increasing investment in high-ROI networking approaches while eliminating activities that don't produce measurable value.

Chapter 29: Arguments Against Networking

Let me be blunt. Networking has legitimate problems, and pretending otherwise does a disservice to professionals who have valid concerns about the practice. Some arguments against networking are weak excuses from people who don't want to invest in relationship building. But others raise substantial issues that deserve honest examination.

I've heard every argument against networking during my three decades in business. Some come from introverts who feel overwhelmed by social expectations. Others come from technical professionals who believe their work should speak for itself. Many come from people who've encountered sleazy networking practices and concluded the entire field is corrupt.

These concerns deserve serious consideration rather than dismissive responses about how everyone needs to network. Networking isn't appropriate for every person, every situation, or every career path. Understanding the legitimate limitations helps you decide whether and how networking fits your professional goals.

The Authenticity Problem

The most interesting argument against networking is that it encourages inauthentic behavior. Critics argue that networking requires people to pretend to be interested in others when their real motivation is self-advancement. They claim that networking turns professional relationships into calculated performances where everyone is acting friendly while secretly evaluating what they can get from each other.

This concern has merit. I've attended networking events where the superficiality was obvious and uncomfortable. People delivering rehearsed elevator pitches, asking probing questions about your business while their eyes wandered to more important prospects, and disappearing immediately after determining you weren't useful to them.

These interactions feel hollow because they are hollow. When networking becomes performance art rather than genuine relationship building, it creates exactly the kind of manipulative environment that critics rightfully object to.

The authenticity problem is particularly acute for people who value directness and honesty in their professional relationships. If you prefer straightforward business interactions without social pleasantries, traditional networking can feel like forced socializing that contradicts your natural communication style.

Some professionals are more effective when they skip the relationship-building phase and move directly to business discussions. This approach works in certain industries and with certain personality types. Trying to force these people into networking frameworks can reduce their effectiveness.

The Time Investment Issue

Networking requires an enormous amount of time that might produce better results if invested elsewhere. Critics argue the hours spent at events, following up with contacts, and maintaining relationships could be better used for skill development, service delivery, or direct business development.

This argument has mathematical validity. If you spend ten hours per month networking and generate one qualified lead, you might achieve better results by spending those same ten hours on marketing, product development, or existing client service.

The time investment becomes particularly problematic for technical professionals whose value comes from deep expertise rather than broad relationships. A software developer might create more career value by mastering new programming languages than by attending industry mixers. A researcher might advance further by publishing papers than by building professional networks.

For small business owners and solo practitioners, time spent networking is time not spent serving existing clients. This opportunity cost can be significant when your business model depends on billable hours or service delivery rather than relationship development.

The networking time investment also compounds. Maintaining a network of 500 professional contacts requires a systematic effort that only increases as your network grows. Eventually, relationship maintenance can consume so much time that it interferes with actual work productivity.

The Introversion Challenge

Networking advice often ignores the real challenges faced by introverts in professional environments. While it's true that introverts can network effectively, the standard networking approaches are designed for extroverts and can be genuinely draining for people who process social interaction differently.

Large networking events, cocktail parties, and conference mixers are particularly challenging for introverts. The noise, crowds, and requirement for constant social performance can be exhausting rather than energizing. Forcing introverts into these environments can reduce their professional effectiveness rather than enhance it.

The energy management issue is real and significant. Introverts might perform well at networking events but require substantial recovery time afterward. This recovery time represents an opportunity cost that extroverts don't face.

Some introverts prefer to invest their limited social energy in deep relationships with a few key people rather than broad networks of acquaintances. This approach can be more effective for their personality type and career goals than traditional networking strategies.

The pressure to network can also create anxiety and stress for people who are naturally more comfortable with written communication or one-on-one interactions. Forcing these professionals into group networking situations can damage their confidence and reduce their overall performance.

The Industry Relevance Question

Networking effectiveness varies dramatically across industries, and some fields genuinely operate differently than others. In certain technical fields, academic disciplines, and specialized professions, competence matters more than connections for career advancement.

Research scientists advance primarily through publications, peer review, and demonstrated expertise rather than professional networking. Their career progression depends on intellectual contributions that are evaluated by subject matter experts rather than relationship builders.

Government positions often have formal application processes, testing requirements, and merit-based selection criteria that reduce the importance of networking. These structured environments minimize the influence of personal relationships on hiring and promotion decisions.

Some technical roles in large corporations focus on specialized skills that are more valuable than networking abilities. A database administrator's career might advance faster through technical certifications and demonstrated system performance than through relationship building.

Highly regulated industries sometimes have compliance requirements that limit the role of personal relationships in business decisions. Healthcare, finance, and government contracting often require formal processes that reduce networking advantages.

The Meritocracy Argument

Critics argue that networking undermines meritocracy by giving advantages to people who are good at relationship building rather than those who are best at their jobs. This concern suggests that networking creates an unfair system where social skills matter more than work quality.

The argument has validity in situations where less qualified candidates receive opportunities because of their networking abilities rather than their competence. When hiring decisions favor personal connections over objective qualifications, the result can be lower overall performance and missed opportunities for more capable professionals.

This problem is greater in fields where technical competence can be measured objectively. If a networking-savvy but technically inferior candidate receives a position over a more qualified but less connected competitor, the organization and the profession suffer.

The meritocracy concern also affects workplace dynamics. When promotions and opportunities go to people with better internal networks rather than better performance records, it can reduce motivation and performance among other employees.

Some argue that networking advantages are essentially a form of privilege that benefits people with better social skills, educational backgrounds, or economic resources for attending networking events. This perspective suggests that networking perpetuates existing inequalities rather than creating fair competition.

The Dependency Risk

Heavy reliance on networking for business development creates dependency on other people's goodwill and availability. Critics argue that this dependency makes professionals vulnerable to relationship changes, economic downturns, and industry shifts that can destroy networking advantages overnight.

When your business depends primarily on referrals from your network, you lose control over your lead generation and revenue stability. If key networking contacts change jobs, retire, or face their own business challenges, your opportunity flow can disappear rapidly.

The dependency problem is especially important during economic downturns when networking contacts reduce their own business activities and referrals. Professionals who have invested heavily in relationship building might find themselves without backup lead generation methods during exactly the times when they need them most.

Networking dependencies can also reduce innovation and competitive advantage. When you're focused on maintaining existing relationships and serving referred clients, you might miss opportunities to develop new services, enter new markets, or create unique value propositions.

The relationship dependency can also create pressure to maintain connections with people who are no longer professionally relevant or personally compatible. This obligation to preserve networking relationships regardless of their current value can become a burden rather than an asset.

The Scale Problem

Networking advice often assumes that building relationships will automatically translate into business success, but this assumption breaks down at scale. As businesses grow beyond certain sizes, networking-based lead generation becomes inadequate for supporting continued growth.

A consulting practice that depends on networking might successfully grow to generate $500,000 in annual revenue through relationship building. But growing to $5 million might require marketing systems, sales processes, and business development approaches that don't depend on personal networking.

The scale problem also affects time allocation. Executives and business owners who spend significant time on networking might reach a point where their networking activities prevent them from focusing on strategic planning, operations improvement, and other high-level responsibilities.

Large organizations often need systematic business development processes that can be managed, measured, and scaled rather than depending on individual relationship-building efforts. Networking might be valuable for senior executives, but it can't replace structured marketing and sales systems.

The Measurement Challenge

Networking advocates often claim that relationship building produces business results, but these results are difficult to measure accurately. Critics argue that networking benefits are often overstated because people attribute business success to their networking efforts without considering other contributing factors.

The measurement challenge makes it difficult to evaluate networking ROI compared to other business development investments. If you can't measure networking results accurately, you can't optimize your approach or determine whether the time investment is worthwhile.

Many business opportunities that seem to come through networking might have developed through other channels if the networking hadn't existed. The counterfactual problem makes it difficult to prove that networking created value rather than just providing one pathway to opportunities that would have emerged anyway.

The measurement challenge also makes it difficult to identify which networking activities produce results and which are wasteful. Without clear metrics, professionals might continue investing time in ineffective networking approaches while neglecting more productive alternatives.

When Not to Network

Understanding these arguments helps identify situations where networking might not be the best strategy for achieving your professional goals.

If you're in a highly technical field where competence can be demonstrated objectively, focusing on skill development and work quality might produce better career results than relationship building.

If you're an extreme introvert who finds networking events genuinely draining, you might achieve better results by focusing on one-on-one relationship building or digital communication strategies.

If you're in an industry with formal processes for advancement and opportunity allocation, networking might provide less advantage than understanding and excelling within those formal systems.

If you're building a business that needs to scale quickly, investing in systematic marketing and sales processes might produce better results than networking-based lead generation.

If you have limited time and energy for professional development, focusing on core competencies might create more value than spreading effort across relationship building activities.

The Balanced Perspective

The arguments against networking aren't entirely wrong, but they're also not entirely right. Like most professional strategies, networking has advantages and disadvantages that vary based on individual circumstances, industry context, and career goals.

The key is understanding when networking adds value and when other approaches might be more effective. Some professionals benefit enormously from relationship building. Others achieve better results by focusing on technical excellence, formal business development, or systematic marketing approaches.

The problems with networking usually arise when people treat it as a universal solution rather than one tool among many for achieving professional success. The manipulation, superficiality, and time waste that critics identify are real problems that occur when networking is done badly or applied inappropriately.

Making the Decision

If you're considering whether to invest time in networking, honestly evaluate your situation against these arguments.

Are you in an industry where relationships significantly affect opportunities?

Do you have the personality type and energy for relationship building?

Are there other professional development investments that might produce better returns?

The decision about networking should be strategic rather than automatic. Understand the limitations and challenges and the potential benefits. Then, make an informed choice about whether relationship building fits your professional goals and personal strengths.

Networking isn't for everyone, and that's perfectly fine. Professional success comes through many paths, and the best approach is the one that matches your strengths, industry, and goals.

Recap

Networking faces legitimate criticisms including authenticity concerns, significant time investment requirements, challenges for introverts, variable industry relevance, potential undermining of meritocracy, dependency risks, scaling limitations, and measurement difficulties. These arguments aren't just excuses from people who don't want to network. They represent real limitations that affect whether networking is appropriate for specific individuals, industries, and situations. Understanding these limitations helps professionals make informed decisions about whether and how to invest in relationship building activities.

Exercise

Honestly evaluate the networking criticisms that resonate most with your situation and personality. Consider whether these concerns represent genuine limitations or obstacles that could be addressed through different networking approaches. Analyze your industry, career goals, and personal strengths to determine whether relationship building deserves significant investment compared to other professional development options. Make an intentional decision about networking based on this analysis rather than assuming it's necessary for everyone.

Chapter 30: Why Networking Is Not Manipulation

People who fail at networking often accuse it of being manipulation. They claim that building relationships for business purposes is fake, dishonest, or exploitative. This is complete nonsense. These critics either don't understand what networking is or they're making excuses for their own inability to build professional relationships.

Real networking isn't manipulation any more than making friends, maintaining family relationships, or working with colleagues is manipulation. Its basic human interaction applied to professional contexts. The people who call it manipulation are usually those who tried some sleazy networking approach, failed miserably, and decided the entire concept was flawed rather than examining their own behavior.

I've heard this accusation countless times over the years. People who attend one networking event, pitch everyone they meet, get rejected, and then declare that networking is just using people. These are the same people who think sales is about tricking customers and marketing is about lying to prospects.

Thcy'rc confusing nctworking with manipulation because they don't understand the fundamental difference between the two approaches.

Manipulation involves deception, coercion, and exploitation. Manipulators hide their true intentions, use false information to influence others, and extract value without providing anything in return. They see other people as objects to be used rather than individuals to be respected.

Networking involves transparency, reciprocity, and mutual benefits. Networkers are honest about their professional goals, provide value to others, and build relationships where everyone benefits. They see other people as potential partners and collaborators rather than targets to be exploited.

The difference is obvious when you understand what each approach entails. Manipulators lie about their intentions. Networkers are upfront about wanting to build professional relationships. Manipulators take without giving. Networkers provide value before asking for help. Manipulators disappear once they get what they want. Networkers maintain relationships for years.

I learned this distinction by watching both approaches in action during my career. The manipulators were easy to spot because their behavior was consistently selfish and deceptive. They would misrepresent their qualifications, make promises they couldn't keep, and abandon relationships the moment they stopped being useful.

These people rarely succeeded in business because their reputation for dishonesty eventually caught up with them. Word spread about their unreliable behavior, and they found themselves excluded from professional opportunities.

The successful networkers operated completely differently. They were transparent about their goals, generous with their time and expertise, and consistent in their follow-through. They built reputations for reliability and helpfulness that opened doors throughout their careers.

The manipulation accusation also comes from people who are uncomfortable with the idea that business relationships serve business purposes. They think relationships should be purely social or emotional, and that mixing friendship with professional goals somehow corrupts the interaction.

This thinking is naïve and impractical. Every relationship serves multiple purposes. You might enjoy someone's company while also appreciating their professional expertise. You can genuinely care about someone's success while hoping they'll think of you when relevant opportunities arise.

Professional relationships don't become manipulative just because they have business components. Whether the relationship provides mutual value and whether both parties are honest about their intentions makes the difference.

When I network with other professionals, I'm clear about my goals. I want to build relationships with people who might refer business to me, collaborate with me on projects, or advise when I face challenges. I'm also clear about what I offer in return: my expertise, my network, and my willingness to help them achieve their goals.

This transparency makes the relationship honest rather than manipulative. Both parties understand what we're trying to accomplish together, and both parties benefit from the interaction.

The accusation of manipulation often comes from people who have unrealistic expectations about networking. They think that networking should produce immediate results without any investment of time or effort. When they don't get instant gratification, they conclude that networking doesn't work or that it requires dishonest tactics.

These people don't understand that networking is about building long-term relationships, not executing short-term tricks. Real networking requires patience, consistency, and genuine interest in other people's success. It's the opposite of manipulation because it's based on providing value rather than extracting it.

I've also noticed that people who accuse networking of being manipulation are often those who are uncomfortable with self-promotion or asking for help. They use the manipulation accusation as an excuse to avoid activities that feel uncomfortable or vulnerable.

These people would rather fail in isolation than risk being seen as pushy or self-serving. They've convinced themselves that networking is beneath them or incompatible with their values, when in reality they're just avoiding the emotional discomfort of building professional relationships.

The irony is that these same people often complain about their lack of business opportunities while refusing to engage in the relationship-building activities that create those opportunities. They want the benefits of networking without doing the work, then blame the process when they don't get results.

Authentic networking is the opposite of manipulation because it requires a genuine interest in other people's success. You can't fake this interest for long. People can sense when you're really trying to help them versus when you're just going through the motions to get something from them.

This authentic interest is what separates networking from manipulation. Manipulators pretend to care about others as a tactic to get what they want. Networkers care about others because they understand that mutual success creates the strongest professional relationships.

Networking creates value for everyone involved.

When I refer business to someone in my network, both the referred client and the service provider benefit.

When I make introductions between people who can help each other, both parties benefit.

When I share industry insights with my network, everyone becomes more informed.

This value creation is the opposite of exploitation. Instead of taking value from others, networking creates new value that didn't exist before. The relationships themselves become assets that help everyone involved achieve better results than they could accomplish alone.

The critics who call networking manipulation are usually people who tried transactional approaches and failed. They attended events looking only for what they could get, pitched their services to everyone they met, and wondered why people avoided them.

They confused networking with sales, relationship building with lead generation, and mutual benefit with one-way extraction.

When their selfish approach failed, they blamed networking rather than examining their own behavior.

Real networking requires emotional intelligence, patience, and genuine concern for others. These qualities are incompatible with manipulation, which requires deception, selfishness, and disregard for others' interests.

The people who succeed at networking understand this difference. They invest time in understanding others' challenges, look for ways to help without expecting immediate returns, and build reputations for reliability and generosity.

These professionals don't need to manipulate anyone because their approach creates willing partners who want to work with them. They generate opportunities through the value they provide rather than through deceptive tactics.

The networking-as-manipulation accusation is ultimately a cop-out used by people who don't want to do the work required to build professional relationships. It's easier to dismiss networking as unethical than to admit you're uncomfortable with relationship building or that you've been approaching it incorrectly.

If you think networking is manipulation, you either don't understand what networking involves or you've been doing it wrong. Stop making excuses and start building genuine relationships based on mutual value and respect.

When you approach networking with authenticity, transparency, and genuine interest in helping others, the manipulation accusation becomes irrelevant. You're not trying to trick anyone or extract value through deception. You're building professional partnerships that create value for everyone involved.

Recap

Networking is not manipulation because it involves transparency, reciprocity, and mutual benefit rather than deception, coercion, and exploitation. Critics who call networking manipulation usually either attempted transactional approaches that failed or are uncomfortable with relationship building for business purposes. Real networking requires an authentic interest in others' success, creates value for all parties involved, and builds long-term partnerships rather than extracting short-term gains. The manipulation accusation is often an excuse used by people who don't want to invest in relationship building or who have unrealistic expectations about networking results.

Exercise

Examine your own attitudes toward networking and identify any concerns about manipulation or authenticity. Consider whether these concerns are based on actual networking experiences or assumptions about what networking involves. Reflect on successful professional relationships in your life and analyze whether they involved mutual benefit, transparency, and genuine interest in each other's success. Compare these positive relationships with your networking approach to identify areas where you might improve authenticity and value creation.

Conclusion

Networking changed my life twice. The first time was when I learned it could save my career during that Friday night crisis at Trader Joe's. The second time was when I discovered it could launch a completely new career when I became a writer.

Both times, the transformation happened because I finally understood what networking is. Not schmoozing at cocktail parties or collecting business cards at mixers, but building genuine relationships with people who can help you solve problems while you help them solve theirs.

"Nothing liberates your greatness like the desire to help, the desire to serve." – Marianne Williamson

---

This understanding took me decades to develop, cost me countless opportunities, and required learning from embarrassing mistakes and painful failures. I wrote this book so you don't have to make the same errors I made or waste the same years I wasted.

The principles haven't changed since I started my career, and they won't change in the future. People do business with people they know, like, and trust. Everything else is just tactics and tools that support this fundamental reality.

You can master every networking technique in this book, attend every industry event, and use every modern tool available, but if you don't focus on building authentic relationships based on mutual value, you'll fail. Networking success comes from consistently helping others achieve their goals while they help you achieve yours.

Effective implementation involves patience, authenticity, and genuine commitment to other people's success. It's easier to chase quick wins through aggressive self-promotion or transactional relationship building, but those approaches don't create lasting value.

The professionals who succeed at networking long-term understand that relationship building is an investment that compounds. The person you help today might refer your biggest client next year. The colleague you stay in touch with might become the key to your next career opportunity.

But you can't keep score or expect immediate returns. You help people because it's the right thing to do and because it creates the foundation for mutually beneficial relationships that provide value for decades.

Some of you will read this book and immediately start implementing systematic approaches to relationship building. You'll research contacts before events, follow up consistently, and track your networking results. You'll see improvements in your professional opportunities within months.

Others will read this book and continue doing what you've always done. You'll attend the same networking events, collect the same business cards, and wonder why nothing changes. You'll blame networking for not working instead of examining your own approach.

The difference between these two groups isn't talent, luck, or natural social ability. It's willingness to treat networking as a serious business discipline that requires systematic effort and consistent execution.

Networking isn't a personality contest. Some of the most successful networkers I know are introverts who prefer one-on-one conversations to group events. They succeed because they understand that networking is about providing value to others, not about being the most charming person in the room.

You don't need to be naturally outgoing to build valuable professional relationships. You need to be genuinely helpful, consistently reliable, and authentically interested in other people's success.

The tools and tactics will continue evolving. New platforms will emerge, technology will advance, and business communication will change. But the fundamental principles of relationship building remain constant.

Focus on the fundamentals: help others before asking for help, follow through on commitments, stay in touch consistently, and measure your results. Master these basics before worrying about advanced strategies or sophisticated tools.

The biggest mistake you can make after reading this book is doing nothing. Networking knowledge without action produces zero results. The second biggest mistake is trying to implement everything at once and overwhelming yourself with complexity.

Start simple. Choose one networking principle from this book and implement it consistently for the next month. Maybe it's following up with every new contact within 48 hours. Maybe it's asking "How can I help?" in every networking conversation. Maybe it's attending one targeted event per month instead of random networking mixers.

Build the habit of systematic relationship building before adding complexity. Once consistent networking becomes part of your routine, you can expand your approach and sophisticate your methods.

Track your results from the beginning. Count the quality conversations, business referrals, and meaningful relationships that develop from your networking efforts. This data will show you what's working and motivate you to continue investing in relationship building.

Remember that networking is a long-term strategy, not a quick fix. You might not see dramatic results in the first few months, but consistent effort compounds. The relationships you build today will create opportunities for years to come.

The professionals who succeed in business understand that everything is ultimately about relationships. Technical skills get you in the door, but relationships determine how far you advance and how much you achieve.

Your network is your net worth, but only if you build it correctly. Focus on creating genuine value for others, maintain relationships consistently, and measure your results systematically.

The principles in this book work. I've used them to build a successful consulting career, transition to a completely different industry, and develop relationships that have supported me through major career changes and business challenges.

Thousands of professionals have applied these same principles to advance their careers, grow their businesses, and create the professional opportunities they wanted. The approach works if you work the approach.

Stop making excuses about why networking doesn't work for you or your industry. Stop waiting for the perfect time to start building relationships. Stop treating networking as something you'll get to eventually when you're not busy.

Start now. Start simple. Start with one person, one conversation, one follow-up message. Build the habit of relationship building and expand from there.

Your career and business success depend on the relationships you build with other professionals. This book has given you the roadmap. Now you need to do the work.

The choice is yours. You can continue struggling with random networking efforts that produce inconsistent results, or you can implement systematic relationship-building approaches that create lasting professional success.

Choose wisely. Your future depends on it.

Appendix Interviews

Interview with Mark O'Donnell

The following interview with Mark O'Donnell, founder and president of RGA Networks, provides real-world examples of the networking principles discussed throughout this book. Mark has built one of Florida's largest business networking organizations and offers practical insights into how networking works in practice.

Richard Lowe: I'm here with Mark O'Donnell, the President of RGA Networks, and I'm interviewing him on the purpose of networking, why people should network and the advantages of doing it.

Mark, thank you for coming.

Mark O'Donnell: Thank you for having me Richard; it's an honor to be interviewed by you.

Richard Lowe: Thank you. So, let's begin by talking about you and your background.

Mark O'Donnell: I'm Mark O'Donnell, President and founder of the networking organization called RGA Networks. A lot of people want to know what RGA Networks stands for because in the networking community and world, a lot of the organizations use lettered acronyms.

The letters RGA mean Revenue Generating Activity, because I believe, as salesperson and a business owner myself, that what you should be doing during business hours is activities that create revenue, or you should be doing tasks that become revenue-generating activities.

I have a broad-based work background. I moved to Florida in 2002 for two reasons. We wanted to move down while we were young enough and while we could enjoy Florida, and to get away from the Midwest cold.

We moved to a beautiful coastal town called Dunedin, which is a beautiful place to visit. A year later we moved to Clearwater, where we have lived for the past eleven years.

I worked for over fifteen years for the National Museum of Transport in St Louis, Missouri. It's a transportation museum; they have one of the largest collections of antique automobiles, trains, and planes in the world.

After moving here, I took a couple of sales jobs and realized the necessity of networking because of the ability to meet and connect with a large group of individuals who can help introduce future clients.

Richard Lowe: Explain to me what you mean by networking.

Mark O'Donnell: Networking is connecting with like-minded, positive thinking individuals, to share their contact and referral database.

For example, suppose my neighbor asked me, "My wife and I are thinking of repainting our house. Mark, do you know of any painters?"

I would say that I don't personally know of any but let me ask my network if they have anyone to refer. I would stand up in a room of the twenty or thirty attendees and ask, "Hey, my neighbors are looking to get their house painted. Who do you know?"

Networking is like a strong word of mouth referral. Because several things start happening when you make that request. One, a person who eats lunch with me – they're usually weekly meetings, often very regular meetings – is not going to give me the name of painters that they don't know, like and trust.

And then they're going to tell that painter that this is for their friend from their networking group. So, when I introduce them to my neighbor, he's going to more than likely get the job because it's a word-of-mouth referral, "Hey, Mark has recommended this guy to paint our house."

Someone in the group will usually come back with a referral, someone they know, like, and trust. I'll pass that person's name over to my neighbors. Since it's a personal reference, they assume (rightly) that they can trust him.

If anything goes wrong, I'm going to then go back to the person who recommended the painter and say, "Hey, your friend didn't do this, this and this and the neighbors are not happy."

Hopefully the way humans work, that painter will want to keep his customer and the guy who referred him happy, that he will fix whatever was wrong and it won't become an issue.

Richard Lowe: You used a term "know, like and trust." Can you explain that a little more?

Mark O'Donnell: You need to know somebody and know that they have the talent that you seek for them to do your task. You wouldn't go to an auto mechanic to get your hair cut, nor would you go to the beauty salon to get your oil changed.

So, you must know them, you need to know that they know the craft. A lot of time that comes with documentation: they've graduated from a university or trade school that has taught them the way to do what needs to be done. Sometimes it's based on experience or testimonials from others.

Following that, you must like someone to want to do business with them. It's a very strong factor; it's almost 90% of your decision. If you felt that you've had a bad experience at a big grocery store, you probably don't shop at that big grocery store as often as you would if you felt you liked the people there.

Finally, most importantly in the "know, like and trust" factor is the trust. The trust is where the money floats from your hand into the other person's hand, because you trusted that they changed your oil and put your car back in working order and you can now safely go travel the roads.

You trust that when the lady spins you around in the chair in the hair salon that you're not bald. You trust that the baker who baked your kid's birthday cake, that that cake's going to taste good and won't be filled with metal shavings.

If people know you and like you, but they don't trust you, they're not going to give you their money.

Richard Lowe: Can you give an example of that?

Mark O'Donnell: I needed to get my car detailed. I hired a guy and he did an okay job but he wasn't the world's best detailer for the price that I paid. I thought it should have been a very good job.

In conversations with other friends, they had had a similar experience. We just chalked it up to experience or lack of caring or something like that. I won't choose to spend my money with him again, because I've found a place that will detail my car to my specifications, and it's less expensive.

Thus, I didn't trust that guy to detail my car again because of how it turned out the last time. The sad thing for that guy is that he no longer gets my referrals when somebody says "Your car always looks so nice; how do you keep it that way?" Instead, I send him to the place that is less expensive and does a better job.

Richard Lowe: Do you have an example of one that worked well for you?

Mark O'Donnell: One referral that worked well for me would be you, for instance, Richard. My friend was looking to get their LinkedIn profile updated; I guess they were getting back into the job market.

I told you about it and you two connected. When I followed up with him I asked, "How is Richard doing?"

He said, "Oh my God, he's fantastic, he's really doing a great job",

I thought, "Good", so you're in my book when somebody needs a writer, a content writer, or LinkedIn information.

Richard Lowe: Well, thank you. You used another word there, "referral". Why don't you explain what that means?

Mark O'Donnell: There's a lead and a referral. A lot of people get those two confused.

I tell people I send flowers when people are alive. I don't believe in sending flowers to funerals, because the people that you love and cherish that have passed on are already dead.

So, I like to send the flowers when they're alive. I look for a florist that thinks outside the box. When I ask for a referral – I like to use locally owned, small businesses – I say something like, "I have friends in Illinois; does anybody know a florist in central Illinois?"

Someone will answer, "Yeah, I know Jacqueline, a florist."

"Great, you know the owner. Do you have her cellphone?"

"Yeah, here's the number."

"Do you mind if you call her to tell her I'm going to be calling to order some flowers for my aunt who lives there?"

"Yes, I will."

That takes the referral a step further. Jacqueline is now aware that you have referred her to me, so you're going to be bringing her business. Jacqueline is going to take a whole lot better care of me than if I was just Joe Schmoe walking in off the street, because Jacqueline will now want to impress me and she'll want to impress the one who referred me to her.

When asked how that referral worked out with Jacqueline, I'll either say, "Oh my God, I loved her", or, "She was the worst florist in world, quit recommending her."

A lead is when you ask, "Does anybody know a florist?" and somebody goes on their phone, gets three names and numbers, and gives them to you.

Those are leads, there's no connection, there's no, "Hey, my friend Richard Lowe said I should call", they'd most likely answer, "Who?"

Richard Lowe: How do you start a conversation with someone you haven't met before?

Mark O'Donnell: First, you introduce yourself. Just walk up, shake their hand, look them in the eye, and say something like, "hello, my name is Mark."

If you want, you can ask someone you know to introduce you, but don't overcomplicate it. People make it too complicated. Just go over to them and introduce yourself. Simple.

Richard Lowe: Okay, then what??

Mark O'Donnell: I get the conversation going by saying something like, "tell me about your business and where do you think it's going?" That always gets someone talking.

Next, "How did you get to where you are today?"

Now, it's best to give them something, "Who could I introduce you to?" Usually that's a great way to get people to like you right way. You're offering to give them something and it's easy.

Finally, don't forget this one, "May I follow up with you? Do you prefer email, text or phone?" Always ask this. Some people use email, others like to be texted, but some hate it, and others want you to call.

Richard Lowe: I want people to email.

Mark O'Donnell: See? So, you ask. It's polite and it shows you respect them by communicating in the way they want.

Richard Lowe: Cool. I interviewed Ron Sukenick and he said one of the most important things about networking is that you give more than you receive. Would you say that's true, and, if so, why?

Mark O'Donnell: Absolutely. I think you must give without the expectation of receiving. It's sort of a karma concept. And I think it was Brian Tracey who said that the more people I help, the more people will help me.

It's like we have two ears and one mouth. I try to give twice as many referrals to my referral partners as I expect to receive back. I know, after doing this for so long, karma is good and the world of reciprocity is amazing.

There'll be days when I say, "Gosh, I really need to pound the pavement and fill my pipeline", and I have two or three people call me saying, "We have two people interested in joining."

The world of karma just sent me several strong referrals that I can then follow up, and see what questions they have about RGA. So, in answer to your question, I think that in life, anything worth doing is worth doing well.

Richard Lowe: I see how it works. You've talked about RGA a little bit, how about telling me more about why you started RGA and where it came from?

Mark O'Donnell: I've always been a big fan of connecting. At the museum, it was very important, when you were restoring cars, or trains or planes, to get the right, passionate professional to do the restoration.

You can be an auto body repair shop, but if you don't know how to work with fiberglass, for instance, then a lot of the corvettes wouldn't be your forte in restoring, and if you don't know how to work with a material, you're probably not going to be as passionate about it as someone who is a fanatic about sports cars.

It's the same way with networking. Connecting people has always been my passion. I did it in the museum by connecting vendors. If we had a good souvenir, I could call the Zoo and tell them, "I'm sending over this manufacturer's representative because they have great pricing on children's t-shirts and souvenir pencils. Would you be willing to see him if he stops by?"

Ninety-nine times out of a hundred they would see the representative as a personal favor to me.

When I moved to Florida I looked at a lot of networking opportunities such as the Chambers of Commerce and seat-specific networking groups, meaning there's only one plumber, one hair salon, one pest control.

There are groups where networking kind of feels like a second job, where if you miss a meeting they kick you out, if you have no referrals they kick you out, if you're late they slap your hand, and sort of embarrass you, so it really felt like a second job.

Then there was a free group, and those people would come and go as they saw fit; I never felt like I got a significant referral passed to me. What I felt was that these people were trying to sell me or recruit me to sell their products or services, which is kind of a far stretch of networking – that's not why we're there.

We're there to promote our businesses. So, one day I decided that we could create a happy median of a networking group where we don't have to be seat-exclusive, where we don't have to require attendance, and I think if you provide value to the members they are going to show up and bring referrals with them.

I always say to people, "The best way to get a referral is to give a referral." Because it's part of human nature to pass it forward. In other words, if I do something nice for you, you'll pass it along to the next person.

Sometimes the universe seems to have a scoreboard; if you've done 10 nice things, the universe is going to reward you by people doing nice actions to you.

That's how RGA was born.

We were sitting there, watching these other poor people who, they didn't bring a referral,

For example, one lady was late because her daycare didn't open on time and she had to sit and wait because she couldn't leave her children alone.

When she arrived at the meeting late, they humiliated her by passing the "late arrival coffee can" and she had to come up with $3.50.

Her morning already wasn't going well. She got to the daycare, it wasn't open, she had to wait for them, she had to drop off her kids, then she saw some poor lady on the side of the street, reached into her purse and pulled out her only five, and gave it to the lady.

Then she gets to the networking meeting and not only is she humiliated for arriving late, but she had to give $3.50 to the coffee can. She couldn't because she, "Just gave it to this lady side of the road, who said she needed it to feed her family."

Richard Lowe: That would be the last time I attended that meeting.

Mark O'Donnell: It was the last time she attended. You want to help, I hope RGA creates an environment where people really want to help each other.

Mark O'Donnell: These organizations, they have many strengths. One of the powers in making it mandatory to attend is you get the people who are very dedicated to the group.

For example, the lady we were just talking about, she was dedicated to the group. It was just the combination of bad events that all happened in one day; she had to borrow five dollars from somebody to pay the $3.50 fine, because the lady who opened the daycare center was late due to an emergency.

Instead of saying, "We are so glad you're here, we were worried about you, usually you're never late." Instead, it was "you owe a fine because you were late."

Richard Lowe: Okay, now describe a typical RGA meeting.

Mark O'Donnell: We wanted to do something different. So, when we first started, this whole concept was newly created and not practiced here in the Tampa Bay market.

Since then, people have copied our format, so I guess it's a form of flattery. The team leaders arrive early so they can get up and greet and introduce themselves to the new arrivals, especially first-timers. We want them to feel very welcome.

The meeting usually begins with, "Why we RGA." It's what makes us come back week after week, after week. A lot of people say they RGA because of the flexibility, they RGA because they can go to any meeting in the area, they can present their business to the RGA members at every one of our chapters.

We have a world-class website; it's 99.99% Google verified, meaning Google will trust the content from our website, along with our business directories. We are often able to get our members on the first page of Google under the categories they choose, which is huge for attorneys, writers, pest control, things that have a lot of competition. Those people know, if you are on the third page, nobody goes to page 3.

Our meeting agenda is standardized throughout our chapters, so if you attend a meeting you will experience the same order of things. It is structured but still allows for some flexibility on the part of the chapter directors. One thing we encourage during the meeting is for our members to have MOMs and DADS. We have our own language in RGA. MOM means meetings outside of meetings. DAD is discussions after dinner.

We encourage our members to meet outside meetings so they can get to know one another and to understand what makes them tick.

This goes back to that "like, know, and trust" factor. For example, if you meet somebody and you know that their business is the sole supporter of their household, they are probably going to be very serious about it.

I think having MOMs and DADs is crucial to the success of the network. People will say, "Richard does that, you really need to have a MOM with him. He just doesn't do coloring books".

Richard Lowe: Tell me more about a MOM.

Mark O'Donnell: A MOM should work – other organizations call them one-on-ones – we like to be a little more creative. These meetings are to get to know each other.

I want to find out what led you to where you're at now. Why are you in advertising, a sales person, or in talk media, and what got you to this level.

How many brothers and sisters do you have? Where did you grow up? What is more important to you, work or home life? You might be sitting across from the next Bill Gates or Warren Buffett, or Vera Wang. The only way you're going to know that is by asking questions.

"I work in advertising but my passion is I make all my own clothes."

You say, "What?"

"I make all my own clothes. I really want to be a designer in New York."

Now you are armed with more information. It is to get to know people on a deeper level. I ask, "How do you like to have your referrals passed on? Do you want me to call you, text you, email you? What is the best way for me to get you contact information of people who want you to reach out to them?"

I also explain my process. If I send you a referral, they know about you and are either expecting your call, or if the person doesn't feel comfortable with that, I give them your contact information so you know that they're supposed to call you.

Often, I try to get their cell phone number, because if you get a call from a cell phone, at least for me, and I don't recognize it, I let it go to voicemail so I can see what the person wants. But if you know that that is the number of the referral you are going to pick up.

Richard Lowe: Contrast a good MOM with a bad one.

Mark O'Donnell: A good MOM is where we get to know each other. We talk about where we're from, how many brothers and sisters we had, what kind of pets we had, what makes us tick, why do we get up in the morning and do what we do. Knowing people's lives is critically important.

Just to earn money is a good why, if you are earning money so your little kids can follow you in the path of attending an Ivy League school, you know that that person is really going to work.

They also ask questions about how they can help you. A good MOM goes both ways. You split the time, be it 30 minutes or an hour. For 15 minutes, they talk about themselves, for the other 15 minutes they ask you questions.

A bad MOM is when someone comes with both their sales brochure and their laptop, and they begin with their sales presentation on why their product or service or whatever is going to help you.

A lot of networkers say that this is the best way for them to explain what they do. I've never found one of them at the end that closes the laptop and says, "Do you know anybody that that would help?"

They usually always ask me is this something I'd like to do. And then I say, "Really, we are not here to sell each other, you're here to educate me so when I am out working with somebody and they say, 'I'm not feeling very well, I wake up with a stiff neck all the time.' I say, 'oh my gosh, I found somebody who has a product that is specifically for people to wake up at stiff necks. Let me give you her name and number and you give them a quick call'."

That is a bad MOM, if they try to sell you. And sometimes if I'm interested in a product or service I'll say right then, "Pull out your calendar, I'm interested, but today's meeting is just for us to get to know each other. So, I would like to see what you can do from me, but because I'm usually time constrained, I don't have the time to extend my MOM by another 30 minutes or an hour."

Richard Lowe: Let's say you meet someone and he's in business and he's not a member of RGA, what do you tell him to get him interested in joining?

Mark O'Donnell: What I say to a lot of the people I meet, is that I represent some of the finest business owners in the area and I would love to invite you to a breakfast or lunch or whatever, or one of our happy hour meetings.

"I think these people are good business connections that can only help you in your business. I sometimes say that I'm in a networking group and there is not a problem in business that we cannot solve collectively. I'd love to connect you to my partners.

What day of the week are you typically free to meet for lunch?" And if they are free on a day that our chapter is a distance away, I offer to come by and pick them up so we can have a conversation while driving to the chapter that is far away.

I always say to people, "You must strive for consistency." I used to do stupid little puns, like, "Networking is a lot like Catholicism. You must show up for mass to get the full facts. If you want to be liked and known, you should be a regular at the meetings.

You can miss a few meetings here and there, most people will say, "Gosh, is everything okay? We missed you last week.' But if you consistently go to one of the chapter's, people at another chapter would say the same thing."

Richard Lowe: One of the things that always gives me trouble is when you get a reference that you don't particularly want. You are not interested in following up with this person because it's not the kind of business you want to do, or they are not the kind of people you want to do business with. How do you handle that?

Mark O'Donnell: What I say is, "I really appreciate you thinking of me but that isn't really a fit from me, there is probably someone else in the RGA that could really utilize that referral to its fullest opportunity."

Richard Lowe: For example, I don't do resumes. That's not something I can do well, and I get a lot of those and I really don't know how to say, "Sorry, this is not what I want to do."

Mark O'Donnell: When you are out networking, find someone who is good at writing resumes and say, "I get asked a lot to do resumes, would you have any problem with me sending you the people I get for resumes? How do you want me to do that? You want me to email you, only to give you a text, how so you want me to connect you?"

Then if they say, "Yes that's great, what can I do for you?" "Well, you know I'm very good at LinkedIn profiles, I'd appreciate you passing your LinkedIn profiles to me. Or, if you come across one that stumps you, then send it to me. I also do ghost blogging; every business owner needs a ghost blogger."

Then you say, "Resumes aren't really my thing, but this person is really good." My other advice is to stay organized, and use your time effectively. I think the networking meetings are very important, you get to see a lot of people in a short amount of time.

But when you schedule these MOMs, schedule them before or after the meeting. A lot of people will say, "Let's do 3 o'clock at Starbucks." Well, you have already blocked the time either for breakfast or lunch, maximize your time opportunities and do it right after the meeting or right before it.

Then follow up, follow up, follow up. As simple as, "Thanks for seeing me today, I learned a lot of great information. You can text that, email that, all those things are very acceptable forms these days."

But follow up. Because then you know that they have got your information. What I try to do is send a week later a more formal follow-up.

I always try in the next 30 days, to get them some sort of result from a meeting. An article I thought you might enjoy, an informational news clip, or something of the web, or a referral. It plants the seed.

I like to think of networking more like farming, rather than hunting. If you need a sale to feed your family by Friday, go hunting and make a sale. But if you want to cultivate a garden of ongoing, continuous referrals, you need to network.

The thing is, and I'm a farmer by nature – you can't just plant seeds, water them, and then walk away. You have to come back to make sure the seeds have sprouted, if they are vining beans you have to make sure there are poles for them, if it's carrots you have to make sure the stalks are growing right and that they are getting enough nutrition. But once you do, the harvest just keeps coming and coming. The abundances there if you work it.

Richard Lowe: That brings us to the end of the interview. Do you have any closing words?

Mark O'Donnell: I always say to people that you are the five people you surround yourself with, and the more people you surround yourself with, the more people you can connect with. We may be born alone and we may die alone, but we travelled the journey called life with other human beings. So, surround yourself with positive, like-minded individuals and cast your net for more business. Networking works when you work it, and I always tell people to network abundantly.

Interview with **Ron Sukenick**

Networking Expert and Author of "Networking Your Way to Success"

Richard Lowe (RL): Tell me about your background and how you got into networking.

Ron Sukenick (RS): I grew up in New York and spent 17 years in the music industry in Los Angeles, marketing for major recording studios. I had a unique ability to get out and connect with people - always loved being around people. I moved into networking back in the mid-70s because it made sense to me. In 1988, I began the expansion of what's now known as BNI. We called it "the Network" back then, and I brought it to Indianapolis.

RL: How did you first start connecting? Were you always connecting with people?

RS: I started my first business when I was five years old in the Bronx. I would ask neighbors if I could take their garbage to the incinerator. Each person paid me 10 cents a week - I ended up with 12 clients. That was a lot of money for a kid. I just loved people. I understood early on that some people move at a faster pace than others; some are people-oriented, some are task-oriented. I get energy from people.

RL: Several networkers tell me the core of networking is "how can I help you" rather than "what can you do for me." Would you agree?

RS: Absolutely. It goes back to the basic concept of reciprocity. When you give to people, it triggers serotonin in the brain - that makes people feel good. I'm a giver, and unfortunately, a lot of the world is made up of takers. Giving is like an investment working for me over the years, like a savings account. If you invest in giving, there comes a time when you can withdraw the support you need from others.

It's all about those eight magic words: "I know someone that can get that done." That's where the money is. We have to continue to look for ways to be useful and resourceful to others.

RL: Can you explain more about that connection concept?

RS: A network is a system of elements - people that link together with common goals. The power is clearly in the connection. A connection is not just between you and me - it's between you and I and something else. I'm always looking for that something else. Whether we both love the Miami Dolphins or we both love the Beatles, there's something.

I become the most interested person in the room, not the most interesting person. What they have to say is more important than what I have to say. People are more vulnerable today than any other time in history - they're open and approachable.

RL: What's your view on traditional networking?

RS: Networking, in my opinion, is dead. I said it in 2004 when my second book came out. It's awkward, hit and miss, situational, always lacks support, and it's never about you.

If I ask 100 people in a room "how many of you are here to sell something?" everybody would raise their hand. "How many of you are here to buy something?" Most people don't raise their hands. There's clearly a disconnect.

The only thing left is to go after relationships. It's so much more fruitful when I go after relationships instead of sales.

RL: How does LinkedIn help business people get ahead?

RS: LinkedIn is the largest professional database in the world - 433 million people worldwide, about 128 million in our country.

The number one activity on LinkedIn is searching for people. So either you're searching for people or people are searching for you.

In my opinion, LinkedIn is underutilized and misunderstood. I got on LinkedIn in May 2004 - I was one of the first 200,000 people worldwide. Most people don't understand why they're on LinkedIn. You have to have a completed profile, get it optimized, and develop a connection strategy.

RL: What shouldn't you do with LinkedIn?

RS: The biggest mistake is they don't use it. You can't just accept connections - you've got to engage with people. Don't confuse activity for accomplishment. Using it incorrectly is trying to sell people right off the bat. You connect with someone and immediately try to sell them stuff.

I believe you have to go from high tech to high touch. The suggestion is to go from connecting on LinkedIn to a face-to-face meeting at Starbucks.

RL: Why do you think people are afraid to ask for help?

RS: They don't want to impose on people. They believe everybody is busy, and they think there's nothing for them to offer in exchange. But what they're bringing to the table is an opportunity for somebody to help them. When we help people, it makes us feel good.

There's this concept of a "who network" - who in your life are you neglecting? The people most people neglect are the people closest to them. Everything you need to accomplish in life, you can get done with the help of people you already know.

RL: Any closing thoughts?

RS: Networking is a place you come from; it's not a place you go to. It's not something you do sometimes and in some places.

It's something we can do all the time and everywhere. You become a giver. You look for ways to become resourceful and useful to people. The more people I meet, the more opportunities I have to help others. That's it - no mystery behind any of it.

Note

Ron Sukenick, president and founder of the Relationship Strategies Institute, passed away in 2022. Ron embodied the principles he taught: building authentic relationships that created real value for everyone involved. As a speaker, business coach, and author of "Networking Your Way to Success," he helped professionals and organizations move beyond standard networking practices to develop genuine connections that improved their bottom line. His generous spirit and practical wisdom left a mark on the business community. The networking world lost a champion when Ron passed, but his legacy of authentic relationship building continues to inspire professionals everywhere.

About the Author

Richard Lowe spent thirty years building networks the hard way before he figured out what works.

As Director of Computer Operations at Trader Joe's for twenty years, Richard managed the technology infrastructure supporting a $16 billion retail operation with 474 stores and 38,000 employees. His networking failures cost him opportunities, wasted time, and nearly derailed his career during a critical system crisis when he had no one to call for help.

That wake-up call forced him to learn networking systematically. He discovered that successful relationship building isn't about personality or schmoozing. It's about providing genuine value to others, maintaining consistent follow-up, and building trust through professional competence.

Richard has applied these networking principles across two completely different careers. In technology, his network helped him solve complex technical problems, hire talent, and advance from individual contributor to senior executive. When he transitioned to professional ghostwriting, he used the same relationship-building strategies to build a successful writing business from scratch.

As The Writing King, Richard has ghostwritten over 50 books for clients including Fortune 50 executives, tech entrepreneurs, and industry leaders. His ghostwriting success shows the power of networking: clients find him through referrals and relationships rather than advertising or cold outreach.

Richard's client outcomes include $30 million in venture capital secured, TEDx speaking opportunities, traditional publishing deals, and speaking fee increases of $5,000 to $20,000 per engagement. These results happen because Richard's network connects him with high-quality clients who trust his expertise.

He has appeared on over 55 podcasts, hosts his own show "Leaders and Their Stories," and has been a guest speaker at

Purdue University's entrepreneurship program for four years. His book "Focus on LinkedIn" became a bestseller, selling 15,000 copies in three days and reaching #43 in all Kindle sales.

Richard's networking expertise comes from real-world application, not theory. He has built and maintained professional relationships through major career transitions, industry changes, and business challenges. His approach works whether you're an introvert managing technical teams or an entrepreneur building a creative business.

The principles in this book are battle-tested through decades of relationship building across multiple industries. Richard learned to network by making every possible mistake, wasting countless opportunities, and gradually developing systematic approaches that produce results.

He currently lives in Florida where he continues ghostwriting for clients who find him through his professional network. His success proves that authentic relationship building creates sustainable business growth regardless of your industry, personality type, or starting point.

Richard believes everyone has valuable professional relationships waiting to be built. The challenge isn't finding the right people. The challenge is becoming the kind of person others want to help succeed.

Books by Richard Lowe

See books by Richard Lowe at
https://masterofworlds.com

Get free publishing insights and industry updates at
https://thewritingking.substack.com

For ghostwriting and book coaching services see
https://thewritingking.com